When to Do What:
A Step-by-Step Guide
to the College Process

Copyright © 2017 Joann Korte Elliott / College Counseling Tutoring, LLC

ISBN-13: 978-0-9991065-0-1
LCCN: 2017951040

Design and typesetting by sanandserif.com

When to Do What:
A Step-by-Step Guide to the College Process

CCT

College Counseling Tutoring, LLC
"It's all about FIT"

Joann Korte Elliott

TABLE OF CONTENTS

Introduction

Many years ago, I met our school's new learning consultant. As she addressed our faculty for the first time, she asked us to close our eyes and, in our minds, drive from our home to a popular area mall. When we were finished visualizing our trip, she asked us how we had gotten there, and the answers were varied. Some had taken different interstates, and some took the back roads. One even walked there. Her message to us was that when students learn, there is more than one way to get from Point A to Point B and there isn't a 'wrong' way to learn just like there was no one way for us all to get to the mall. I've used her analogy countless times when working with families in the college admissions process. There is no one way. There is no right way (while there are certainly preferred routes). So many people are concerned about image, doing it right, and not making a mistake along the way. The process of finding your way to college, though, is a journey.

During nearly a quarter of a century working in secondary education, I met with well over a thousand students and their families to discuss their hopes and dreams for the student's future. Despite their enthusiasm about the future, many were fearful and lost at some point in the journey. While undertaking a new chapter of life, change is exciting and fresh. At the same time, it can also be daunting, overwhelming, and scary. In addition to the intimidating cost of attending college and figuring out how to pay for it, by far the largest concern I saw was people's need to understand the process... where do I start, when do I do what, and how do I get organized. Many came to my office and confessed they "knew nothing" about the college process and simply asked, "when do I do what"? I could see some measure of their success would come from their sense of order and control over this lengthy process. Most felt behind at some point (even if they weren't) and some compared the college process to a roller coaster ride both emotionally and physically.

I left the traditional secondary educational setting to go into private practice for several reasons. Among those was that I saw the role of a high school counselor wearing so many hats that they were essentially becoming ineffective on all levels by no fault of their own. As it relates to the college process, counselors handle so many other tasks that their ability to spend quality, individual time with students is greatly diminished. In some states, student to counselor ratios average 800:1. Currently, in my private practice, I work with families individually so they may schedule as many appointments as they need to get them where they want to be and they can take the time needed to have a clear understanding of the college process. But, I have also come to realize not everyone can afford, access, or has the time for private counseling on an ongoing basis. I saw a need to make a resource available to those who just wanted to work the process on their own and simply needed a guide to help them. From this realization, *When to Do What* came to be. In addition to a large volume of information, also included in this book are many of the worksheets that I use with my clients in our sessions to help them get organized, reach their goals, and be successful. Helping others reach their goals has always been the driving force of what I do. Writing this book and by putting an order to the college process for those who "know nothing" has allowed me to put what I've learned after years in the trenches out there for anyone who would like a better understanding of what the college application process entails.

I wrote this book for over-scheduled families, those who need some extra hand-holding, those who home-school, those without counselors within their high schools, as well as high school counselors and college admission offices seeking a resource for their students. My hope is that this book will be an empowering resource for designing bright futures for high school students as they continue their educational journeys.

This book is designed to be straightforward and simple. This book isn't about getting into a specific type of school (though the same basic steps apply to everyone). If you are the student, this book will coach you through what you need to do to recognize your dreams and will teach you how to get there efficiently, affordably, and on time. If you are a parent or educator, it will provide peace of mind that you are doing everything possible to empower your students.

DISCLAIMER: Please note this book is designed to be a *guide* and is not all-inclusive. It will give you general direction, and an overview of the process, but is not designed to give information on every single scenario you might encounter in the college process. Because the journey to college is different for every student and their family, you are encouraged at various points in the book to enlist the help of other professionals who have expertise in a specific area. It is ultimately the family's responsibility to be proactive in the student's college process and self-advocate. This book is only one piece of the information-gathering you will need to complete the college search and admission process successfully.

MY PHILOSOPHY ON COLLEGE

Before you delve into this book, I want to make one thing clear. My philosophy is that college is all about FIT. If you don't have a good fit, it is never going to work. I liken it to shoes. Shoes can be as fancy, expensive, and as name brand as you like but if they don't fit well, they will surely end up tossed to the back of the closet and never worn. College is the same way. You want college to fit well. It should be a place that is comfortable and fits well, but also one that can stretch you academically, socially, emotionally, and professionally. Like a good pair of shoes, college should give you a lot of miles. And, like a good pair of shoes, a little room in the toe to grow into them. Keep this in mind when you're out visiting colleges, and you come across that one that just feels 'right.' That intuition is something to be heeded.

When it comes to college, it is important you run your own race. For some reason, in today's society, we associate distance to a school, the name of the school, and the subsequent price tag as status symbols and markers for success. I hate to break it to you, but just because a student gets into a great school doesn't mean they will be more successful or a better person. A person's character and integrity have little, if anything, to do with where they went to college. Colleges are full of cheaters along with drinkers, partiers, and those who sleep all day. Why are they more successful than the student who lives at home, goes to the local community or four-year college, and is working a part-time job to pay their way through college? The difference isn't where the student goes as much as who they are and the work ethic they possess. Only then can the school be an effective tool in molding a strong and successful individual.

It's so important you find a college that is not only a fit academically and socially, but also financially. I cringe every time a family apologizes that their kid can't go to school 'X' because they don't have the money. Don't apologize! If you've raised a great person with a great work ethic, you've done a great job! College is all about FIT. What works for one student doesn't work for another. Rather than following the herd, follow the beat of your own drum. I have seen families take second and third mortgages to finance their kids' educations. Doing this only accomplishes two things: students live clueless as to what it takes to finance an education and, secondly, it only delays the financial burden when their parents are strapped at retirement, can't take care of themselves, and need to move in with their adult children.

You need to be smart with your money. You've worked too hard to do otherwise. College tuition rates inflate at a rate much higher than the cost of living does. And since our raises are often based on a cost of living rate, it makes sense that college is exponentially more expensive than our income can allow. With that said, there are options out there and ways to not put 'all your eggs in one basket' financially or regarding admission, and we will discuss those within this book.

My advice to you throughout the college admission process is to start early, follow these step-by-step directions to get yourself organized and follow your gut. If, during your college search process, you determine that technical school, starting at a community college or some other path is the best fit for both student and family, DO IT! We often get caught up in keeping up with the Joneses and worrying about how we look in the eyes of our classmates. Do you think your classmates will care when you go to School "X" only to find it's not a fit and you are miserable? Or, when you are buried in debt and too afraid to admit it, and it is compromising your life? No. Keep your eyes on your own page. Find your own FIT. Run your own race. Work to become the best version of yourself possible. You got this! No apologies or explanation needed.

HOW TO USE THIS BOOK

This book is designed to be simple. Its purpose is to walk you through the college admission process step-by-step whether you are a parent or a student. With that said, it is not all-inclusive. That means you most likely will need to enlist the help of others at different points along the way, such as your high school guidance counselor, private college counselor you are working with, or your admissions and financial aid representatives from the colleges to which you are interested in applying, just to name a few. For this reason, you will be encouraged at different points in this book to seek out additional resources to help you along the way. We've all heard the expression "it takes a village to raise a child." It is certainly true in the college process as well.

This book is a first step guideline, intended to help a broad scope of readers. If you intend to apply to Ivy League schools or other elite universities, do keep in mind that you may want to seek additional help from professionals. This book will provide you with foundational knowledge about the application process rather than specific advice regarding certain universities. I encourage everyone who is reading this book to read it cover-to-cover once to get a full understanding of the process at a glance and then re-read sections as you work your way through the timeline and the action steps.

This book is divided into three sections. The first five chapters comprise Section I and answer all the broad QUESTIONS people generally have from "When do I start talking about college?" to "What if I don't know my major?" While I recommend everyone read these chapters, if you are already well-versed on the topic you can certainly skip a chapter. You will find an Action Step box at the end of the chapters in Section I that summarizes the chapter and gives you pointers on things you need to do regarding the topic discussed.

Section II of the book (chapters 6-11) is geared specifically towards ACTION. These are the chapters that explain the process and tell you when to do what in an organized, step-by-step manner. Section II literally walks you through the process in an orderly fashion and outlines the timeline of the college process. To simplify the process as much as possible, each of these action-based chapters has two boxes. The first box comes at the beginning of the chapter and is a timeline box. This box will give you the range of WHEN you should be doing this particular step. (Keep in mind that steps will overlap. As an example, you may be working on testing while also visiting colleges.)

The second box you will see in Section II will come at the end of each chapter. This will be an Action Step box. This box will summarize the chapter and tell you what to do to complete this part of the college process. Reading this book without taking action will get you nowhere! These helpful Action Steps are similar to those I use with clients in an individual session. They are productive in moving the process along, and because they are broken down into baby steps, it makes the process much more manageable and less overwhelming for both parents and students. Some may argue my timelines start too late. While you can certainly start some action steps earlier than indicated, some are less flexible like when to do the actual process of applying for admission or filing for financial aid. The reason I put the timelines where I did is that, in my experience, most people do not work on things when they are supposed to and are playing catch-up most of the time. Therefore, I put in what I feel are *realistic* timelines versus ideal ones.

The final section of the book is reserved for special circumstances and for providing additional information. Chapter 12 addresses special circumstances for those who are athletes, performers, those who want to take a year off, or have learning issues that may need to be considered. Again, if none of these scenarios apply to you, feel free to skip this chapter. Following Chapter 12 is additional information including a glossary, a list of websites, and books that might be helpful to you.

Lastly, you will notice many chapters have worksheets or other handouts that will help you with the process. (The worksheets are designed to be cut out and can be hole-punched and put in your binder so you can keep all your information in one place.) Because my goal is to EMPOWER students, you will find handouts and worksheets that are geared to put the student in the driver's seat. Teaching independence on the way to adulthood starts now. The worksheets will guide students on how to construct emails or have conversations with admission representatives. They will also help them track data and become organized. This is a book for anyone who has never embarked on this journey as well as those who want to learn more or do things differently than before. Keep in mind this book is designed more like a WORKBOOK, so the idea is that you can use it, cut it up, write in it and highlight key terms or instructions. By the end of your college search, your copy of this book should be well used! Let's get started!

Section 1:

Questions Most People Have About College

CHAPTER 1

When Should We Start Talking About College?

When to start talking about college varies from student to student. I have worked with families where parents called me as early as a month after the student started freshman year (way too early) to those who have called me as late as March of the student's senior year (despite my many attempts to get things rolling much earlier). Ideally, the sweet spot lies somewhere in the middle. Maturity has a lot to do with when you start the college process. And when I say start the college process, I mean having meaningful conversations about what the future might look like. The college process is a long one. While you might begin talking about college at the end of the student's freshman year as you work to choose classes appropriate for college admission, the discussion about testing or about the process of applying to specific universities comes much later.

If you are a parent reading this, I want to address a few things as it relates to having a conversation with your student about college. As you start to talk about college, there are a few ways the conversation can go, and timing is everything. It can either go appropriately, as planned, or it can blow up in your face. Other than working to pick good classes for the following year, I say: leave most of the college discussion dormant in the freshman year. Some may argue this opinion, but the reason I stick to this is that transitioning to high school is hard enough.

Freshmen have a difficult enough time making new friends or finding their locker let alone having the discussion of college and where to go after high school. Let freshmen be freshmen. Let them use all their brain power and energy to focus on the social and academic changes that high school brings. There is an incredible amount of learning that takes place during this time socially, as well as academically, and allowing them to live in the present moment and learn those life skills like time management, self-advocacy, and personal responsibility are key to being successful later in their educational careers. There is no point in skipping steps. Figuring out the college process by the end of the student's 8th-grade year does nothing to score points in the admission process. Let kids be kids. If you want to help your student be prepared for college,

I urge you to read Chapter 2 which addresses two things you should do from the moment they start high school to encourage success later. So many students of mine would come in sobbing about pressures from home to 'get into a good college' when all the student wanted to do at that moment was get their history project done and study for the biology test they had the next day. Timing is everything. Choose your timing wisely.

So how do you start that conversation? First, make it light and casual. Inquire rather than pressure. Show interest rather than lay out an agenda. Show support rather than serving up that lecture of "When I was your age..." As adults, we all would have chosen to make some different choices as we look back on our younger selves. Whether it be to not procrastinate or take that teacher up on the offer of help, we see the error of our ways. Hindsight is 20/20. But, mistakes or poor choices also help us learn. I say this all the time: Failure is a GOOD thing. The maturity children demonstrate at 15 is not the maturity they will show at 25. They will learn, and sometimes it will be the hard way. Regardless, this is their life to navigate and as much as you want to fix everything, you can't. And if you try to control or handle everything for them, you are doing them a HUGE disservice in the long run.

The initial discussions about college should be casual, yet productive ones. One that helps the student identify things they know they want and reveal areas that are overwhelming or scary for them. The conversation with a student should start in simple terms...Do you want to go to college? If so, two years or four? Do you want to go to trade school instead? Do you want to live at home? Live in a dorm? Do you know what possible majors or careers might interest you? You are not asking for a list of colleges or majors, but what characteristics they would like to see in the next chapter of their educational life. I think a lot of students are scared and, quite frankly, not ready to leave home for college for the first year or two. I've seen many students force themselves to do something they're not ready for and ultimately drop out and come home. It's a blow to the ego and often sets them back further than if they'd stayed at home the first year or so and gradually worked their way up to living in a dorm or out of town.

This conversation should also be ongoing. One discussion about a "wish list" of what a student wants should not be engraved in stone. We all change our minds from time to time. So long as the student knows what the questions are, he or she can have a change of heart as knowledge about different options becomes available. If you start this conversation with your student midway through the sophomore year, you have nearly a full year (if not more) to tweak the wish list and define a clearer picture of what your student wants.

And, if you are the student reading this book, I have some advice for you as well. I encourage you to let your defenses down when working with your parents during this process. Many students come to me and are frazzled by the onslaught of never-ending questions from their parents about college (insert eye roll here). It usually happens around dinner time or holidays or the night before you have a huge project or test and have zero time (or interest) in such a monumental discussion. Rather than blow up or stomp off, schedule a time for a weekend or day when you know you can commit the time to the discussion and then put a time limit on it. If you discuss college for 30 minutes every 3-4 weeks when you are a sophomore, you can make great headway by the time you get to junior year. Now, it all depends on what your goals are too. If you are aiming for the top of the top, it's going to require more time and energy. Here's the bottom line: your parents, even though they drive you crazy, truly want the best for you. Although you are sure to argue, keep in mind that you're playing for the same team. You and your parents both want you to get to college successfully. You both want your success and happiness. You both want this to be as painless as possible so when you have these talks, just remember that you're working for the same goal, and do your best to tackle this in that manner.

ACTION STEPS
for Chapter 1

WHEN SHOULD WE START TALKING ABOUT COLLEGE?

1) Decide WHEN to have that initial conversation about college. (If the student is a junior or senior then there is no WHEN— the time is NOW.)

2) Set rules as a family as to when college should not be discussed and then choose what works for EVERYONE involved. (Do you avoid dinner time, after 9 pm, the night before tests, etc.?)

3) Come to a mutually agreeable day, time and location of where and how those conversations about college will happen. (Ex: Second Sunday of the month, from 3:00-3:30 pm)

4) Always leave the discussion with a plan for the next meeting—Do phone calls need to be made, research done, etc.? Homework will most likely be involved for both parent and student. WRITE DOWN those homework items, so both parties are accountable.

CHAPTER 2

What Can I Do in High School to Get Ready for College?

Even if the actual process of searching for a college doesn't begin until later in high school, there are two things students need to consider from the moment they begin their high school career that will impact their ability to go to college. The first is to consider the courses the student is enrolling in each year. The second is to consider the extracurricular activities in which the student is involved.

THE IMPORTANCE OF CHOOSING APPROPRIATE COURSES IN HIGH SCHOOL

Academically speaking, what courses a student does (or doesn't) take is important in the college admission process. Each college has different criteria of what they recommend and/or require as part of their admission process. Some colleges, for example, require a fourth year of Math (all classes being Algebra I and higher) or two years of a foreign language to be admitted. Your high school's graduation requirements will probably be loosely defined based on your state public college's admission requirements. But, remember that your flagship university (big state school) or an elite private institution may require more rigorous curriculum requirements for admission.

So, what do you do? First, read your high school's curriculum guide, so you have a full understanding of what courses are offered and what prerequisites are needed to take them. Then, when registration comes around, speak with your high school counselor or adviser. They know the overall admission requirements for colleges and can guide you on which classes you need to take that will put you in the best position to be admitted to college. Any course that is a remedial course will slow you down some in reaching your goal.

As an example, math can often throw some students a curveball. Let's say the student moves into freshman year and only tests into an Introduction to Algebra class, while the majority of students in freshman year are in Algebra I. Being in the lower level class will slow down the path for the student's subsequent years of math because, as we all know, you can't skip steps in math. Although not ideal to be in a remedial class because it slows the progress, it is important to go that route to get the foundation. If you want to get your student to "catch up," then meet with the school counselor to see what local resources could help them not only get the foundation needed but also to advance to where he or she wants to be and is required for college.

I have often seen well-meaning parents try to appeal a recommended course so their student can 'advance' to a higher-level math. In most cases, this tactic backfires. What ends up happening, in the end, is that the student might be allowed (against the better judgment of teachers and counselors) to take a higher-level course. The parents are happy, but they soon find their student is struggling and in over their head. The problem is now we have a student who may be in the 'right' course, but failing miserably and that grade will be a permanent part of the student's transcript. Remember that school is about LEARNING and not just checking off boxes. It isn't uncommon for a student to be a little deficient in one area. Better that a student LEARN the material and have a good foundation to move to the next course than to push them along with no mastery ever taking place. That will never serve them in the long run and college will be a struggle. You will simply be delaying the inevitable. High school students who are the most successful academically concentrate on a few things:

1. SUCCESSFUL STUDENTS TAKE COURSES THAT ARE APPROPRIATE TO THEIR ABILITY LEVEL. These include courses that challenge but do not overwhelm them. This may be a mainstream class for some, an honors course for another. Some students need the intro class to set the foundation to succeed and build their skills. Don't try to impress by 'over-taking' a class just because it looks better. School is about learning. I'll remind you again: Run your own race. Don't worry about somebody else's class schedule, test scores, or GPA. You will do just fine by doing your personal best.

2. SUCCESSFUL STUDENTS TAKE MULTIPLE CORE CLASSES THAT ARE REQUIRED FOR COLLEGE ADMISSIONS. Courses like math, science, social studies, English, and foreign language should make up the majority of a college-bound student's high school schedule. This still leaves room for an elective course or two for fun each year that the student would enjoy taking or even a study hall! Believe it or not, colleges don't care if you take a much-needed study hall. If you are taking a tough course load and playing a sport or working a part-time job, you may need to take a study hall rather than fill your schedule to be successful in all of your undertakings. This leads me to the third thing that academically successful students do.

3. SUCCESSFUL STUDENTS CREATE BALANCE BETWEEN THEIR COURSEWORK AND HOME LIVES. Not every class is labor intensive. They branch out and explore classes that pique their interests, make them think, and allow them to use their creative side. These classes might include oral communications, computer programming, art, or band to name a few. Colleges neither expect nor want a transcript full of honor level courses with all A's. While grades and courses are important, having a balanced skill-set is far more important. College admission representatives have repeatedly told me they prefer a well-rounded student with some B's who knows how to advocate for themselves or is passionate about an elective subject or exhibits behavior of being a lifelong learner to the student who has the 'perfect' transcript but doesn't know how to accept criticism, rejection, or know how to problem-solve. Perfection isn't necessary (or possible) in the college admission process. Yes, there are some schools that want that, but for most admissions processes it is a holistic review and one that expects shortcomings in one area and successes in another. It's part of being human. And I'm pretty sure we all check that box.

Now that you understand the importance of taking challenging, but appropriate courses and fulfilling core course requirements, you can pick courses that reflect your abilities and interests as a student. I strongly encourage you to talk with your counselor from the moment you enter high school about your goals while you work towards picking appropriate courses. (Is college in the plans for you? Trade School? Military?). Because course selection is a domino effect, and prerequisites are often crucial to getting into the next level of the course the following year, it's crucial you read your high school's curriculum guide so you can map out the trajectory of your education. That doesn't mean you will always make the grade to take the next course in the sequence, but you need to set yourself up to be appropriately challenged but not overwhelmed. This will open the most doors for you when considering college.

THE IMPORTANCE OF BEING INVOLVED

Choosing your high school classes wisely is only half of the puzzle when setting yourself up for future success. Remember I mentioned that colleges like well-rounded students? We've all heard the expression "All work and no play makes Jack a dull boy." We can't focus on the academics all the time. So much learning about ourselves, how we work as a team, collaborate, problem-solve, time manage, and take risks comes from both the classroom and from extra-curricular activities. The first year or two of high school should be about exploration. Join a club, try out for a sport, or take a risk in auditioning for a choir or play. Try new things. You may find something you love that you'd never been exposed to previously. Colleges expect your first year or so of high school to be especially exploratory.

They understand if you took a chance on the robotics club as a freshman and didn't pursue it your remaining years because you fell in love with theater instead. High school should be a time of discovery and finding out more about who you are and what your interests are. When you are a freshman, sign up for a club or two your first semester if you're not already playing a sport. This will help you not only figure out what you like and don't like; it will help you meet people outside of the classroom. And feeling like we are part of something and being connected with friends is extremely important in high school.

Activities don't always have to be school-sponsored clubs or sports. You might have a part-time job, play select soccer, or be in a community play. Those things all count as part of the activities you will report on your college applications. One thing to always remember is that when it comes to activities, quality always trumps quantity. You shouldn't be aiming for a laundry list of a million clubs and activities that you can list on your activities list or resume. Instead, you should be aiming for a list of a few activities that are near and dear to your heart. Or, dare I say, passionate about doing.

No one expects you to be involved in 10 clubs if you play a sport that eats up most of your after-school time. Not everyone is cut out to be in theater or speech club or to sing in the choir. The goal is to figure out, over the first year or two, what you enjoy and then focus your energy on that. As an example, let's say your freshman and sophomore year you join the robotics club, Spanish Club, the community service club, and the sound crew for theater. Over time, you figure out you are most passionate about doing community service and love theater. Focus your energies there and let the others go.

Activities should be progressive, and you should take on more leadership roles the longer you are involved. So maybe over time you become the head of the sound crew by junior or senior year and show new students the ropes. Or, maybe you become more focused on your community service work, which leads you to do more in-depth service at a hospital during which you discover your love for the medical field and ultimately leads you to pursue a college major in nursing. The bottom line here is: do what you love.

Write down your activities and years of involvement as you go along through high school. It will make reporting your activities on your application much easier when the time comes. I'll address how to put together an activity list or resume for college admissions later in this book, but it's important you know out of the starting gate that being involved in extracurricular activities in high school is crucial to your overall education. You can't go backward and become involved after the fact. Don't miss the bus on this one. Get out and start exploring!

ACTION STEPS
for Chapter 2

WHAT CAN I DO IN HIGH SCHOOL TO GET READY FOR COLLEGE?

1) Read your high school's curriculum guide to have a full understanding of the courses offered and prerequisites needed to enroll in various courses.

2) Meet with your high school counselor or adviser early on in your high school career to make sure you are choosing the correct courses to ensure your eligibility for college AND your ability level. Continue to meet with them regularly throughout high school. PLAN AHEAD!

3) Do your best academically. Grades do make a difference in the college application process.

4) Remember you are here to LEARN. Don't over-enroll in a class that is too difficult or take classes that are too easy for your ability level.

5) Get involved in high school! Join clubs, play sports, or volunteer. Get a part-time job or join the theater! Do what you enjoy!

6) Write down all your extracurricular activities and years of involvement as you do it. This will make reporting your activities to colleges easier when the time comes to apply. (You will find a form to help you keep track of your activities at the end of Chapter 9.)

CHAPTER 3
What do Colleges Look at in the Admission Process?

As you begin to undertake this process, it is important you have a clear understanding of what colleges are looking for in their applicants. Most people are in the dark on this one or find it mysterious or elusive, but it's rather straightforward. There are half a dozen pieces of information colleges MAY consider when making the admission decision, and you'll be happy to know that standardized test scores are only one piece of that puzzle. In addition to testing, the other components that may be up for consideration in the admission process include:

- The student's grade point average (GPA)

- The rigor of the courses the student took in relation to the curriculum the high school offers

- Activities the student was involved in

- The student's essay and/or interview

- In some cases, the interest the student has demonstrated in the college or university.

Let's break down each piece and see how it affects the admission process and what you can do to make yourself more marketable.

A student's GPA is a major contributor in their acceptance to a college. Obviously, the higher the grades the better. However, some students and parents mistake this as "straight A's" and this isn't the case. Colleges look at cumulative GPA, yes, but they also look at trends in grades as well. So, it's not only important to have the highest grades as you can, but also a consistent pattern to your grades. As an example, let's say you had a rough start your freshman year. Adjusting to high school was tough (or you weren't connecting the dots on how important school is) and you barely pulled C's. But, as the years progressed, there has been an obvious uptick in your grades. That demonstrates to a college that your grades have steadily improved as you have gotten used to the demands of high school and have shown a consistent pattern of improvement.

Most colleges are okay with this so long as the growth and improvement are there (and the initial grades weren't too low). The flip side of this coin is the student who starts off with straight A's in their first year or two then lets their grades drop their last year or two. Slacking off is not a good trend and colleges will be able to see this in just one quick glance at your transcript. Slacking off is hard to hide. You definitely want to reflect the first scenario here and not the latter.

What if, though, you've had one bad semester in high school due to extenuating circumstances? You had mono, a concussion, were in a car accident, were hospitalized for depression, or you had a family member die? Life events can impact your grades (and attendance). If you have such an extenuating circumstance, you can explain it to the admissions committee by answering the question on the application that asks if there is anything else you'd like the admission committee to know about you. It's not for excuses, but for justifiable circumstances that explain a deficit in your attendance or grades. If there is no such question on the application, you can always include a letter of explanation or give your admissions representative a heads-up so they have the complete picture.

*In addition to a student's GPA, the colleges will also look at the **rigor** of the courses a student took while in high school.* If a student has taken lower level courses when they were qualified to take higher level or honors courses, it gives the impression that the student did not challenge him or herself. How will a college know the caliber of a student's curriculum?

When a student applies to a college and requests a transcript be sent, the high school will also enclose a profile of the school. This profile is a synopsis of the high school and gives the college a 'snapshot' of the school. Information included on a high school's profile include the basics such as enrollment, accreditations, and administrators, as well as academic information such as the highest level of courses offered in each subject which might include Advanced Placement (AP) and honors courses. (An Advanced Placement course is one that offers college-level instruction and a standardized examination that, based on the students AP test score at the end of the semester, may award them college credit or advanced placement in a given subject.) By providing this information, a college can easily see by comparing it to the student's transcripts what caliber of classes the student took. Now, colleges don't expect that you have all honors courses, but if you have straight A's but never tried to challenge yourself by taking an honors course it may raise questions to the admission staff. There are colleges that might not look at rigor, but the more difficult the college is to get into, the more likely it is they will scrutinize the caliber of your courses. Most students may take a more challenging curriculum in some subjects and not in others. If a student has an affinity for English and social studies but not math and science, it's logical their transcript will reflect more difficult courses for the former rather than the latter.

There are two scenarios that relate to curriculum and rigor that people will ask about all the time. The first is: *What if my high school limits the number of honors courses a student can take each semester?* If a student is qualified to take five honors courses, but only enrolls in four because school policy dictates limitations, the colleges will be aware of that limitation because that stipulation will be dictated on the high school profile that is submitted with each student's transcript. Then, the college understands the student may have only enrolled in four honors courses that semester because the school has limited the quantity of honors courses they can take.

The second scenario I am asked in relation to rigor is: *If the high school doesn't offer honors or AP courses will it negatively affect the student in the admission process?* The short answer to that question is *no*. Students cannot control the offerings by their high schools and so it can't be held against them in the admission process if they didn't have the opportunity to take a more rigorous course. Some schools are in rural areas or are very small schools that don't have the enrollment to offer some courses. Instead of holding it against the applicant, colleges will look at the course load the student took in relation to what was offered at the school.

The bottom line with rigor is NOT that the student tries to enroll in as many honors or Advanced Placement courses as they can, but to take *appropriate* courses where the student will be challenged and yet not overwhelmed. Remember that the focus of education is LEARNING. This means balance in coursework and extracurricular involvement. It is often tough to take a multitude of honors courses that require loads of extra homework and play sports or be the lead in the school play. I've seen many wise students take one fewer honors course to give themselves the extra time they need to keep their head above the water in all areas of their lives. For those who think they will take everything offered because it will help them get into a better college, I can tell you I have seen it backfire more often than not with the result being tears, anxiety, depression, becoming overwhelmed, and shutting down not to mention lower grades. No college is worth your mental sanity. Listen to your school advisers, teachers, and counselors when they try to help you create a balanced schedule. They have your best interest (and your sanity) at heart. They know what the curriculum entails along with your abilities and potential for growth. They can often see down the road and know what skill sets will be required to succeed in a course. They can help guide you to a challenging, yet balanced course schedule where you can and will succeed.

As I mentioned in the previous chapter, a student's **extra-curricular involvement** is another area colleges will consider as part of the admission process. Those activities can come in the form of school-sponsored activities such as clubs, sports, and theater or those outside of school including volunteer work, part-time jobs, scouts, or community-based sports or theater. Colleges need to see there is more to your life than just school.

Colleges want students who are not only going to contribute to their classroom discussions but who also will add to the life on their campus outside the classroom by getting involved in the many activities college offers. Remember that schools like depth in a student's activity list. Again, what this means is quality trumps quantity. A student's multiple-year participation in an activity is more important than how many activities he or she participated in while in high school. There is more detail later in this book on how to report your activities to the college as part of the admission process and how to develop your activity list or resume.

The **essay** is the one part of the application process that elicits the most fear in students. This is probably due to the open-ended nature of the essay. The essay is simply another way for the colleges to gather information about students. If you think about it, most of the information on an application is basic reported information such as your name, address, grades or other data about you. The essay gives you the opportunity to express yourself creatively.

What is unique about you? What do you bring to the table? What does the rest of your application not give you the opportunity to share about yourself? Do you have a unique sense of humor or an unusual life experience to share? The essay is one more piece of information for colleges to get to know you. Not every college will require an essay for admission. Larger, public institutions are less apt to ask for an essay as opposed to more elite, smaller or private colleges. Where you apply will determine whether you will be writing a college admission essay. See Chapter 9 on applying to college for more details and tips on writing your essay.

An **admission interview** is one of the lesser-required pieces of the admission process. However, if a school 'recommends' or even lists the interview as optional, I strongly encourage you to consider doing an admission interview. Like the essay, the interview gives you an opportunity to sell yourself to the college and for them to get to know you. You might meet in a room at your high school or make arrangements to meet at your local coffee shop to talk. Having a conversation with your admission or alumni rep works well for the student who may not be a strong test taker, for example.

The interview gives you the chance to have a conversation with the admissions representative and let them see the real you and your glorious personality, not to mention learn about your stellar work ethic and great attitude on life. None of those attributes come through much in the formal part of the application process. Just like with the essay, the interview will more likely be required at smaller institutions where they have the time to have individual conversations with their applicants. You might be interviewed by an admissions rep or by alumni of the college. Either way, the people who interview you often become your advocate in the admission process. It is much easier for an admission representative to go to bat for you and help you with the admission and scholarship process if they can connect a name and face.

I have seen time and again where the relationship between the college's admission rep and the student can have a powerful impact on the student's decision and ability to attend a university. It comes as no surprise that the admission reps who have the best working relationships with student applicants have continually higher enrollment from these students. What doesn't work is the family who calls the admission rep late in the game questioning an admission decision or looking for additional financial aid and they have never met with the rep. It's hard for someone to advocate for you if they don't know who you are! If an interview is not required, but you are seriously interested in the college, ask the admission rep assigned to your school if they would be willing to meet with you. Initiating contact shows your seriousness as an applicant! Use your admission reps. Interview with them. They are there to HELP you!!

Lastly, **demonstrated interest** is a growing piece of the admission puzzle. Because of modern technology, the ability to track data related to the student's interest with a college is becoming easier. Tracked data might include if a student stopped at the college's table during a college fair or visited with the rep at the student's high school or if they've visited campus. All these activities demonstrate the student's interest in a school. This tracked information may give the college a clue as to how serious a student is about their institution. For the student who has been receptive to meeting with the college admissions rep, sending emails of inquiry and participating in campus tours or college visit programs, tracking demonstrated interest might bode well for them. I wouldn't worry too much about this piece of the puzzle. If you've been visiting campuses and talking to reps of the schools you are interested in, you should be fine. To the contrary, a weekly email or call to the rep to express your interest is unnecessary, and it can often become annoying and work against you in the long run.

You will find as you work your way through the application process for each school that some (but maybe not all) of the pieces mentioned above will be required to complete your application. Be sure you know what is required of you for a given school and submit your materials on time. Chapter 9 outlines the college application process in detail and contains an application checklist to help you keep track of what you need to complete each college's application process.

ACTION STEPS
for Chapter 3

WHAT DO COLLEGES LOOK AT IN THE ADMISSION PROCESS?

1) Educate yourself on what colleges may be looking at in making an admission decision including standardized test scores, GPA, rigor, extracurricular involvement, your essay, interview, and demonstrated interest.

2) Determine what is required by each individual school to make your application complete.

CHAPTER 4

What If I Don't Know My Major?

I chose to put a chapter on choosing a major in this book because it is probably one of the most frequently asked questions I get when I meet with families. Not knowing an exact major is one of the most frustrating aspects of the college admission process for students and their parents. Students today still struggle with the age-old question "What do you want to be when you grow up?" just like most of us did. This is the first time students have ever had the opportunity to decide what path their lives will take. For their entire life, someone has told them to go to school each day, and their lives have been largely planned for them. Students today live in a society that has told them they can be anything they want to be. While that may appear to be good news initially, leaving the playing field wide open with endless options is, quite frankly, intimidating.

Students often look at choosing a major as a way of defining who they are and their potential for success in life. In their eyes, it is a make-it-or-break-it moment. It can be a scary decision process because it requires that teens look inward and listen to their intuition. It requires introspection and patience. It is often not something that is an automatic 'knowing,' and it certainly is not something that others can tell them what to do. This is frustrating for teens because they naturally look to their peers for approval and guidance. It is part of becoming an adult. We grow from a child looking to our parents for advice and direction to valuing our peers' opinions. And now, at this pivotal point in life, students worry about what their peers (and adults) will think of their chosen field of study, of what they will become, and how their career choice will affect how people view them. It feels as if the next 40 years of life and employment and their status in society is determined solely by their college major.

One of the biggest arguments I see between parents and students is disagreeing over major. The student may want to major in dance (a 'fluff' major in the parents' eyes), and the parents want the student in the 'practical get-a-job' major (example: business). One way to handle this dilemma might be to double major with a major of interest to the student on one hand and a major with a practical application on the other. The truth is, selecting a college major is one piece of a long series of life decisions. Many people get degrees that have nothing to do with what they will eventually do for a living. It is simply a springboard to open doors. With that said, there is a popular term in college recruitment these days called 'return on investment'. College is an expensive undertaking and families want to know that the money they are spending will help yield a productive career and allow their students to reap the financial benefits of a college education.

College is a huge investment, and some parents worry about why they are spending money if their student doesn't know what they want to study. As one parent told me "attending college without a major is a really expensive way to do career exploration." True, but there are several things that you can do to help narrow the field of potential majors and careers before you enroll. These options include career interest inventories, personality tests, job shadowing, informational interviews as well as strategizing how to select a college based on these results. The key here is starting early. If you are a student starting the process early (say sophomore or junior year), time is on your side. Act on some of these suggestions, and you will help narrow the field tremendously.

If you are later in the game (senior year), any information-gathering is still helpful and knowing possible majors can help you choose a college that is a better fit for you in the long run. If you are interested in identifying potential college majors, these steps can help. Notice I wrote 'majors' in the plural. Rarely do students know exactly what major they want. Having options is always a good idea. Parents sometimes expect their student to have a laser focus on what they want to do and know without any hesitation what they will do. It is unrealistic that a student at 17 or 18 years old knows EXACTLY what they will want to do for a career. Many college institutions I work with tell me their most popular major for incoming applicants is "still deciding." It takes time to figure things out.

The days of working for the same employer for 40 years and getting your retirement watch from the same company you worked at since you were 22 are pretty much over. Any adult who is honest will tell you they struggled in this decision process at least once in their life. What is important here is to always be working. Working at figuring it out, working at the part-time job to make ends meet, working the entry level job (which you may not love), working all the time to make yourself into who you want to be, and working towards making a viable contribution to our world in a way that uses your talents and passions. Working your way up the food chain as it were. While we all have passions and dreams, life is full of hard work. Dreams take time to come to fruition which makes the realization of them all the sweeter.

To help students narrow the pool of possible careers, there are several things they can do. Doing as many of the following suggestions as possible will give additional information and confirmation that they are headed in the right direction. Things to try include:

1. ELIMINATE CAREERS AND MAJORS. Not knowing what a major or career entails is not a good reason to eliminate a career. Knowing you have absolutely no interest or ability for a career is another situation. Everyone knows at least one career field that is of no interest to them and can probably eliminate it. Some may know they have no interest or ability in math, building, and problem-solving and take engineering as a possible career off the list. Others may eliminate certain aspects of the medical field because they can't stand the sight of blood or are uncomfortable around sick people. Knowing yourself and what your limits are can help eliminate the careers you don't want and give contrast then to what you do want. Start to narrow your career and major search by taking two to three majors or careers off the table. This will help to narrow the playing field. It's very normal to switch majors after the first year or two in college, so aiming for the right wheelhouse is perfectly acceptable if you're uncertain. You want to eliminate what doesn't fit then focus on your strengths and play to them.

2. TAKE AN INTEREST INVENTORY. An interest inventory helps people to identify careers they are drawn to based simply on their attraction to certain activities. It does not take into account skill sets or educational prowess. It simply identifies potential careers based on what the person likes to do. Good options for interest inventories include the Strong Interest Inventory (SII) and the Self-Directed Search (one of my personal favorites). You can take interest inventories online or they may be available as part of services your high school offers (ask your counselor). A free online interest inventory is available through O*Net. O*Net is the government-based website that gives information on employment and labor trends. You can take an interest inventory via O*Net by going to www.onetonline.org and clicking on the "I want to be..." link to get started.

3. TAKE A PERSONALITY INVENTORY. We all bring different traits to the table as individuals. A personality inventory can help students (and adults) figure out who they are and how they work best. Certain personalities align with certain types of work and there are some great resources out there to help figure it all out. Personality inventories like the Myers-Briggs Type Indicator (MBTI) identify 16 personality types. You can take a free version of this type of test by going to www.16personalities.com. This website gives a scaled-back version of the personality inventory. If you'd like to take a formal personality test, I suggest you find a counselor who specializes in the Myers-Briggs Type Indicator and use their expertise and knowledge to help you fully understand the results of the assessment. Based on your results, there is a great book titled *Do What You Are* which aligns your personality type with possible careers that might be a fit.

4. IDENTIFY VALUES. Values identification is one area my adult clients often overlook, and I know it is one that high school students rarely consider. What is values identification? It is simply acknowledging what you do or do not want in a career (and in life). As an example, do you want to work in a cubicle? Travel? Dress up for work every day? Have job security? Be creative? Go for the status a job title may bring (doctor, professor, etc.)? Have a flexible schedule? Have routine? Work from home? Work independently? Be around people every day? Work with your hands? Be your own boss? Leave your work at work at the end of the day? Help others? Work weekends and have days off during the week? In other words, what is truly important to you in a job that gives you the lifestyle you want? Let's be honest. You cannot have it all. But you want to consider what is truly important to you to have the life you want.

I once had a student who wanted to be an OB/GYN. Yep. She wanted to deliver babies. She had the interest in the career, and she definitely had the brain power. The problem? She wanted to work weekdays from 9-5. Unfortunately, babies can't tell time. If she wanted to deliver babies, she needed to acknowledge she would be called in the middle of the night or just as she sat down to Thanksgiving dinner. Babies come when they come. She did not want to budge on her schedule. I encouraged her to think through what she truly valued in her lifestyle. If she couldn't budge on her schedule, she needed to consider another aspect of the medical field. Aligning our values to our careers is what keeps us happy in our jobs and our everyday life. Our careers need to align with our values. I've seen more than one person quit a job on principle. Their strong sense of ethics didn't align with their boss' way of doing business, and they simply walked away rather than cheat a client. Know yourself, know what you value, and you will find a career that supports who you are.

To better help you identify what is important to you in life, I have put a Values Identification Exercise worksheet at the end of this chapter to help you brainstorm those things in a career and life that are important to you. Once you identify potential careers based on your interests, go back and see how well your chosen career aligns with your values system.

5. JOB SHADOWING. There is no better teacher than being in the trenches. We can look at videos of people doing jobs all day long. It will never compare to following someone around and see what a real day-in-the-life looks like for a given career. I see college applications all the time where students have an interest in a particular major (let's say medicine), and they include on their resume or activity list several job-shadowing experiences. Some may shadow a pediatrician, a surgeon, and an orthopedist to determine what area of the medical field they want to study. It shows they are serious about learning more about medicine and the on-the-job shadowing helps them narrow their focus.

They may shadow as little as a day or two or as long as a month. It depends on the set-up of their shadow experience. Shadowing gives the opportunity to see what it's like to do a specific job. It's great to shadow before you commit to a field. I have seen many a future teacher get to senior year in college excited about education only to get to their student teaching and hate it! Most schools now put students in classroom teaching situations earlier so they have a greater grasp of what working in the field will be like.

You can shadow in virtually every field, and most people are usually happy to have you tag along for the day. There are a few things you need to remember if you are going to shadow. You are in the real world, which means professional attire, actions, and manners at all times. This means no sloppy dress, no texting or being on your phone, and being an observer and not an interrupter. You are there to shadow, not interfere. Shadowing requires great maturity. If you are interested in shadowing, ask teachers, counselors, friends, or family members who may be able to connect you with someone in your chosen field. Spend a day or two with someone. I guarantee that by the end of the experience, you will have a clearer picture whether or not you can see yourself in this field.

6. INFORMATIONAL INTERVIEWING. Informational interviewing is simply sitting down and talking to a person about their career. It doesn't necessarily have to be done in the work setting. It may be easier for the person to have a one-on-one conversation at a coffee house or other casual setting where you can ask your questions and have them answered without distractions of the job. Informational interviewing also requires a great deal of maturity on the part of the student. If you are looking to do some informational interviewing, there are a few things you need to remember.

First, come prepared with a list of questions that you want to ask. There is nothing worse than awkward silence when doing an informational interview. To help you get started, I've put together a list of questions at the end of this chapter you might consider asking. Questions like day-to-day activities, training required and likes and dislikes about the profession are all good to ask. Secondly, dress nicely. This is not the time for t-shirts and shorts. Your appearance lets them know you are taking this seriously and respect their profession and their time.

Most people are happy to share with others their expertise and experience. Most people are happy to talk to young people interested in what they do and that they can possibly mentor along the way. Don't be afraid to ask someone if they will talk to you about what they do for a living. If they say no, don't take it personally. Simply move on to the next person. Just like with job shadowing, ask friends, family, and others to make connections with people who work in your fields of interest.

7. RESEARCH. Finding additional information and career descriptions on the internet is not the sole means in which I would gather information to make my career and major choice, but it can give great supplemental information on what a career entails including job outlook, salary information, and training needed. It doesn't give the personal aspect that job shadowing or informational interviewing do, but it does give the solid quantitative information that is essential to making an informed decision. Good resources to consider include O*Net (www.onetonline.org) as well as an association's website for professional development. As an example, counselors often belong to the American Counselor Association or the American School Counselor Association. Find a particular career's national website, and you can often find data about the profession.

You might also consider perusing job search websites to see what the salary, job descriptions, and availability are for jobs in your area that you might consider. Let's say you want to be an athletic trainer. Look online at job-related websites like Indeed or LinkedIn and do a search in your area of athletic trainers. Take note of the number of jobs available, where the positions are located (private companies, gyms, etc.) as well as any salary that may be indicated. This might also give some additional information to what careers are viable. Not all jobs are listed online so take that into consideration. It's not a one-and-done approach, but searching job descriptions and employment openings online may be a good supplement as you try to find out more about a given career.

8. VOLUNTEER. Never has there ever been a better form of career exploration than volunteering. Aside from the benefits of giving back to an organization or community, volunteering is a great activity in self-discovery to see what experiences you are drawn to and what talents you bring to the table. Over the years I have seen many students figure out their major by volunteering. It may have been in a hospital setting working with people, in a company organizing files, or working outdoors doing construction or manual labor. Every experience may not be enjoyable, but it does give contrast then to what a student may or may not want in a career. Either way, it is good information and a win-win because you are also bettering the world.

The best thing about volunteering is that you can start young! There are plenty of age-appropriate activities for kids all the way through adults. If you are looking for places to volunteer, consider places you are familiar with like your place of worship or your local hospital. You might also use electronic resources like Volunteer Match (www.volunteermatch.org) to help align you with opportunities in your region. Some communities have their own local database to help you connect with volunteer opportunities. As an example, Memphis has a great program called Volunteer Odyssey (www.volunteerodyssey.com) that matches potential volunteers with organizations needing help. Do a search online for your local community's volunteer opportunities.

If you're trying to figure out a major or at least narrow the options before you apply to college, here is my suggestion. Narrow the field down to three majors. We all have majors we would NOT consider, so take those out of the equation. Then, look at what's left. If someone forced your hand to pick three majors right now, what would they be? Perhaps you would narrow your pool to Business, Nursing, and Psychology.

Find a school that has all three majors. That way, you can change majors without having to change colleges. A word of warning, though: if you are interested in a career that is competitive in the admission process such as physical therapy, nursing, pharmacy, or some engineering majors, I would suggest you get yourself into these tougher majors upfront if possible. It will be easier to transfer out of Nursing and into Psychology or Business rather than the other way around. Remember to ask the question, too, about if you can get into your major as a freshman. (This is called direct entry.) Some colleges don't allow you to apply to some of their programs until the end of your sophomore year. If this is the case, it is a waiting game and one you are not guaranteed to win. If you like your university and don't get into the competitive program for your junior year, would you continue your education elsewhere or change majors? Picking three majors you would consider doesn't solve your career path dilemma, but it does buy you some time. Unless you are in some specific health-related majors (physical therapy, nursing, etc.) and some engineering programs to name a few, most colleges and programs don't require a student declare their major until the end of sophomore year. This allows you time to figure out what program of study you're interested in while still taking your general education courses (social studies, math, science—the courses every school requires regardless of major.) I strongly suggest, though, that once you are enrolled in college and if you still don't know your major, you actively pursue your adviser or career counselor on campus for direction and help in your decision-making process.

The bottom line in all of this is that no one else can tell you what to do with your life. Sure, while someone may be willing to give inaccurate (or unsolicited) advice, this is your life, and you need to run your own race. Even for those of us who have been working for years, there is no clear-cut path. There is a saying that you don't have to be able to see the whole staircase at once, you just need to see the next step.

Students need to be willing to do the tough work and know themselves and their talents. They must make connections with others to move forward and find their way in life. There is no magic bullet or express lane. It is a series of events that include research, introspection, and connecting with others that require action, hard work, and patience. And this information-gathering process will be repeated several times throughout life. Learn this skill set now, and you will be well-equipped to adapt as career changes happen over your lifetime. And, trust me, change will happen.

WHAT IF I DON'T KNOW MY MAJOR?

1) Take an interest inventory.

2) Take a personality inventory.

3) Identify values in a career and/or lifestyle that are important to you.

4) Eliminate careers or fields of study that are of no interest.

5) Make a list of careers that interest you and spend some time job shadowing.

6) Using the questions suggested in this book, conduct informational interviews for careers of interest.

7) Volunteer.

8) If you want to have some focus on a major when looking at colleges, choose three that have the greatest interest to you and make sure the colleges you are looking at have all three majors. That will allow you to change majors after you get there and not have to change colleges.

WORKSHEETS FOR CHAPTER 4

VALUES IDENTIFICATION WORKSHEET

DIRECTIONS: On the left side of the sheet, brainstorm and list the qualities you want in your career and life. Don't try to identify a specific career, just attributes. On the right side of the paper, brainstorm and list the qualities you DON'T want in your career or life. Again, don't try to identify a specific career, just acknowledge what you do not want. Whatever you do, don't overthink any of this, just go! (If it helps, set a timer for 1-2 minutes so it forces you to just list freely.) Don't feel you need to use all the lines. Just write until you are finished!

I WANT/VALUE IN CAREER AND LIFE

I DON'T WANT/VALUE IN CAREER AND LIFE

31

Here is a sample of what your list might include. Use this as a guide, not as items you need to list on your own answer sheet. Don't ever feel ashamed that you don't value things in life you think you 'should.' We all value different things, and you need to find where you can be the best version of yourself and shine.

I WANT/VALUE IN CAREER AND LIFE	I DON'T WANT/VALUE IN CAREER AND LIFE
Helping others	The corporate 'suit'
Job Security	Lots of travel for work
Variety in work hours	Working in sales/making quotas
Ability to have/spend time w/family	High Stress
Pension / 401K plan	Being dressed up for work
Creative freedom	Being stuck in a cubicle all day
Being outside during work day (or after)	Working in isolation
Goal-oriented	Working with young children
Room for advancement	Building anything
Being around people	Math
Supportive co-workers	Lots of work after hours
Leaving my work at the end of the day	Anything to do with sick people
Education-related	Long commute
Writing/sharing information	Research
Time off / vacation (balance in life)	Being on call / working weekends
Solving problems	Making 'tons' of money
Use of technology on the job	Moving a lot for the job
Working with teenagers	Being my own boss/entrepreneur
Being a lifelong learner	Working 3rd shift
Variety of job duties	Meaningless work with no impact
Environmental issues	Manual labor

Name of Interviewee: _____ Profession: _____

1. Tell me about how you got involved in this career and the path your life took to get here.

2. What were you drawn to as a kid/teen as it relates to what you do now? (Hobbies, subjects in school, etc.)

3. How much education did you need to do this job? Where did you go to college? What was your major?

4. What do you like best about what you do for a living?

5. What do you like least about what you do for a living?

6. Walk me through what a typical work day is like for you.

7. If you had to do it all over again, what would you change? Would you choose the same career?

8. What advice do you have for someone like me who is considering this field?

9. What could I expect in terms of starting salary? Job availability?

10. How do you suggest I get practical experience that would help me get a job later?

11. Can you suggest anyone else who works in this field that I might interview who can help me gather more information in this field? (Be sure to get their contact information.)

12. Can I please have your contact information in case I have any follow-up questions? (Ask for a business card.)

Add your own questions here before you go:

NOTE: Always be sure to THANK the person you've interviewed for giving up their time to help you. Also, it is a nice touch to send a handwritten thank you note afterward. At the very least, a thank you email should be sent.

CHAPTER 5
What Resources Are
Out There to Help Us?

This chapter is short and sweet, but oh so important! I can't stress enough the importance of involving people, events, and other resources to help you on your journey to college. The college admission process is a constant learning curve. Even if you are a parent who has helped a previous child with the process, you will find the process is different for every person. Because each student wants different majors, types of schools, and may be a different type of learner, it is essential to arm yourself with every available type of help depending on the situation. If you are the student, you need to self-advocate! Meet people, introduce yourself, and ask questions! Regardless of what direction you are headed, I can recommend six essential resources to help you.

1. **COUNSELOR.** The school counselor is equipped to help you navigate these tricky waters when it comes time to suggesting various colleges that might be a fit for you. They are also indispensable in the application submission process. While you will submit your own application, they will be the ones who submit your transcripts and letters of recommendations to the schools. Forging a positive working relationship with your high school or college counselor early in your high school career will help you with the admission process. The better they know you, the more they can help you, but you must initiate the relationship. Counselors are there to guide and help answer your questions. But, they can't help you if you don't ask! If your school doesn't have a counselor or if you are home-schooled, consider enlisting the help of a counselor who specializes in the college admission process if you feel you need more assistance.

2. **BOOKS.** Great books about the college process are everywhere! From being a good test taker or writing a great essay, books on specific topics about the college admission process are available online through Amazon, your local bookstore, and even your library. While many people like electronic versions of these books, I say go for the old-school print copy if you can. This will allow you to highlight, take notes, and mark up the pages. There is something about putting pen to paper that is so much more real and motivating when you physically write your to-do lists or circle that one crucial piece of information. But whatever way you choose to gather the information, just put what

you've learned into action. To help get you started with a few suggestions of books, see the recommended reading list at the back of this book.

3. ONLINE RESOURCES. Online resources can range from free college search engines like Peterson's or Big Future to specific software programs purchased by your school or district to aid you in the process. You can always google your topic and find an abundance of information on any college-related topic, but be sure to check the credibility of the source. There is a lengthy list of helpful websites at the back of this book to get you started. Check with your counselor to see what other electronic resources they suggest. There is a good chance, too, they will list some of those on the counseling page of your school or district's website.

4. COLLEGE ADMISSION REPRESENTATIVES. Any time you can involve people in your life to help you reach your goals, you are ahead of the game. College admission reps are sometimes the most overlooked and undervalued piece of the admission process. These are the folks who help you navigate the process for their school, answer your questions, give you information about events on campus, advocate for you in the admission and scholarship process and be your point of contact. I am sometimes amazed (or appalled) at how little respect college admission reps get and they do such fantastic work! Introduce yourself to them and let them help you. They can't advocate for you if they don't know who you are. I know a ton of admission reps, and they are the nicest and most helpful people you will ever meet. They are not paid on commission and so aren't trying to 'sell' you on their school. They are looking for individuals who will make their school stronger and for whom their school would be a great fit for the next four years. Use your admission reps! You should know each admission rep for each school you are applying to by name. I believe this is crucial to being successful in the college process. There is a contact log at the end of this chapter so you can record their contact information. Once you know the admission reps you will be working with on a regular basis, add them to your phone contacts. These are people you must know because they can make your life much easier.

5. COLLEGE FAIRS. Thousands of college fairs are held each year so students can meet with admission reps and gather information on a variety of schools. There can be anywhere from 50 to upwards of 200 plus colleges represented at a college fair. The sheer number of colleges can be intimidating, so you'll want to research colleges before you go so you can target who you would like to speak with while you're there. You might also want to register for a fair before you go. While it's not required, it has distinct time-saving advantages. When you identify a college fair you would like to attend you will want to go to a designated site to register for the fair. When you do, you will be asked basic demographic contact information. After you register, you will be able to print (or put on your phone) a barcode that will be scanned by the admission rep of the various tables you visit while at the fair. This will give them your contact information, and it will save you a ton of time from filling out those little information cards by hand! Again, this will give you one more way to get connected with the admission reps and to learn more about the colleges from information they will send you or campus events you will be invited to attend. To find out how to register for a fair, ask your high school counselor, or you can just check out these sites to see if one is handling registration for a college fair in your area:

www.gotocollegefairs.com
www.strivefair.com

6. COLLEGE VISITS. There is nothing like making a decision based on first-hand experience. College visits are the number one way students decide where to attend college! Chapter 8 is devoted entirely to this topic. Everything from what to look at, what to ask, and how to set up the college visit is covered.

ACTION STEPS
for Chapter 5

WHAT RESOURCES ARE OUT THERE TO HELP US?

1) Create relationships with counselors, admission reps, and other individuals so you have a support system when working through the college admission process.

2) Utilize information through books and electronic sites to learn more about schools and various aspects of the college admission process.

3) Take advantage of attending high school-sponsored events such as college and financial aid nights or college fairs to learn more, ask questions, and network.

4) Visit colleges when you are ready, so you can physically see the campuses and make an informed decision!
(See Chapter 8 on visiting for more information.)

WORKSHEETS FOR CHAPTER 5

COLLEGE ADMISSION REPRESENTATIVES
CONTACT INFORMATION LOG

Keep track of each admission representative you are working with so that you can contact them as needed. You might also consider adding them to your phone contacts.

COLLEGE/UNIVERSITY	NAME OF REPRESENTATIVE	EMAIL ADDRESS	PHONE NUMBER

Section 2:
A Step-by-Step Timeline for College Admission

TIMELINE OF COLLEGE SEARCH
AND APPLICATION PROCESS

MID-SOPH–MID-JUNIOR YEAR

Discuss goals and make a wish list of colleges. Use online search engines to help you find colleges that fit your criteria. Visit local schools in sophomore year and extend radius for junior year.

SPRING OF JUNIOR YEAR

VISIT! VISIT! VISIT! This is the number one way students choose their school. Visits should happen spring junior year through senior year.
(Local visits earlier)

FALL/WINTER OF JUNIOR YEAR

Use every research opportunity available...counselors, books, reps, college fairs, etc, to gather information. This process is ongoing!

FALL OF SENIOR YEAR

Completion of most admission applications (and college scholarship applications) should happen between August 1 and December 1.

WINTER/SPRING OF JUNIOR YEAR

Register for first ACT and/or SAT. Ideally testing should begin early second semester of junior year and finish around fall senior year.

OCTOBER OF SENIOR YEAR

Parents(s) should complete the FAFSA which will determine student need and offers in the form of grants, loans, and work study.

WINTER/SPRING OF JUNIOR YEAR

Once preliminary research of schools is completed, contact admissions offices to schedule visits. This can continue through senior year.

BY MAY 1 OF SENIOR YEAR

Student & parent(s) should examine all admission, financial aid, and scholarship offers and commit to one school and decline the others in writing.

CHAPTER 6

Step 1: Figuring Out What You Want in a College

TIMELINE:

SOPHOMORE YEAR – MID-JUNIOR YEAR

(Students may change their goals up until senior year as they learn more about what they want)

THE IMPORTANCE OF FIT

While it is important that you have a clear understanding of what colleges will be looking at in the admissions process, even more important, is what *you* are looking for in a college. FIT is the most important consideration when choosing a college. What is right for one student may not be right for another. By far, the most popular talk I give at high school college nights is the one about FIT and choosing a college. There are essentially five ways your college should fit you. If you can check off all these boxes, there's a great chance you will be happy with the college you ultimately choose.

1. ACADEMICALLY. It is important that you find a college that fits you from an educational standpoint. You want to find a school that you feel comfortably challenged attending. The goal here is to find something that you can be successful at, but not totally overwhelmed. Look for a place that will allow you to stretch and be challenged. On the flip side, don't undershoot the academics so much that you are bored or wasting your time and money because you aren't learning anything. Balance is key here.

2. FINANCIALLY. It's okay to apply to a school that might be out of reach financially in the event they come through with scholarships or financial aid, but don't put all your eggs in one financial basket. You need to apply to schools with a variety of sticker prices. If you know you can't afford a $60K per year school, then pick one or two like that and then choose others that are a third to half that price or less. Or, choose a local school where you'd have the option to commute and save money. Mix it up. I've seen students who think they'll get all kinds of financial aid only to find out too late they don't qualify and then have missed deadlines for other more affordable schools. This backs them into a corner, and their options are slim at this point.

3. SOCIALLY. College will be your home for the next four years, and so it's important you will find some kindred spirits at your new school. Find a place you feel like you connect with others. Make sure it's not too big or too small, so you don't feel overwhelmed or bored. Find a place that offers extracurricular activities you like so you can be involved. While it's good to find a place that will expand your world to meet people whose lives and thinking may be different from yours, you will also need to feel comfortable. Find a place that fits you! That means different strokes for different folks—do you need to feel like you come from the same value system, socioeconomic background, spiritual or religious background? Do you thrive when you are placed outside of your comfort zone and meet all kinds of new people? Do you like to know everyone or be a stranger in the crowd?

4. EMOTIONALLY. Where can you get the mental and emotional support you need? Some students have academic, physical, or mental health issues that they will need continued support for to succeed. Look for a place that gives you the support personnel you need like nurses, health centers, counselors, and tutors. If you aren't supported emotionally, you will never succeed academically.

5. GEOGRAPHICALLY. The location of your school is also crucial. Do you want to be able to get home every weekend or only once or twice per year for a major holiday? Do you want cold or warm weather? A small town or large city? Again, I would consider various geographical distances for college when creating a list of potential schools. I say this because I have seen time and time again where parents and students argue over a distance only to find that, in the end, they prefer to be six hours from home rather than 12. Or, they find out a parent is sick, and they end up wanting an option closer to home. Life unfolds in random ways. Having an Option B is probably a good idea. Better to leave a few doors open in case you change your mind.

Identifying what you want in a college and setting goals can be a tough timeline to pin down. It kind of goes hand in hand with when you get started on this whole process. Students can start setting goals as early as freshman year, but it's likely they will change their minds as they mature and discover what is truly of interest to them. To play it safe, I say goal-setting happens from the middle of sophomore year until the mid to end of junior year. Sometimes, self-discovery and goal-setting roll right into senior year.

So, what kind of goals should you be setting? The kind that help you dream about your future and lead you down a path that will get you to your logical 'next step' in life. When you get started talking about college, have those casual conversations about what the future might look like. As those become a bit more solidified, you have a foundation on which you can build and start to see what schools might be a fit. On the pages that follow, I encourage parent(s) and student to fill out the wish list of what might be desired in a school. Remember, what you think you want can, will, and should change over time as you gather information. This step is merely a starting point to begin a conversation or to take the first step.

There are a lot of questions that students and parents must answer to get pointed in the right direction about school. Students need to determine things such as do I want a two-year or four-year education? Do I want to live at home and commute or do I want to live in a dorm? How far am I willing to travel to get to college? Do I want a public or a private school? To answer these questions, one must understand what the options are and understand the differences.

Before you get started on the worksheet, you may need some information on what some of the options listed are. Here are some explanations of questions asked on the wish list to help you:

2-YEAR EDUCATION. This usually means community college. There are many two-year programs out there that help a student get a solid career off the ground. These might be careers in a tech field (nursing assistant, vet tech, computer aided design, etc.) If you look at an online catalog, you can see exactly what types of two-year degrees (associate) that community colleges offer. You can also look for technical schools for trades like auto body repair, HVAC repair, plumbing, etc. Some community colleges and trade schools now even offer dorm options if students want the full campus life experience. Some people use a community college to "get their basics." This means they take their first two years of general education courses (English, math, social sciences, sciences, etc.) and then transfer them to a four-year school. This is often a much cheaper option since community colleges cost less than traditional four-year schools.

Community college can also be a great stepping stone for students who aren't ready to move directly into the four-year setting either academically or socially and need a year or two to get established first.

4-YEAR EDUCATION. This means a traditional college. Students who graduate from here have a four-year degree (bachelor), and it sets them up for professional entry-level jobs (nursing, teaching, business, engineering, etc.). Many students like the traditional four-year education because they want to have a chance to experience college life in its truest sense. Depending on where you choose to enroll, you can either live at home and commute or live in the dorms when you attend a four-year school.

GAP YEAR. This is when the student takes a year off after graduation to pursue other interests before moving on to college. In most cases, I suggest students apply to college in the fall of their senior year and reserve the right to have the school hold their place and delay entry for a year if they want to take a gap year. Some students spend their gap years working, traveling abroad, improving their learning skills, volunteering, and job shadowing. It is always best to have a specific plan or program in place to do a gap year. If the time spent is not productive, it may actually be more of a detriment as the student may flounder if they don't have enough structure that first year. A gap year should be an enrichment to the student's upcoming education. You can read more about designing a gap year in Chapter 12.

PUBLIC COLLEGE. A public institution is one funded by state and federal tax dollars. While there is still tuition at public schools, the sticker price is often much lower than private institutions. Don't let that fool you though. I have seen some students attend a private school for less money because the private schools can have deep pockets with institutional money that allows them to be generous with scholarships and financial aid. Public schools tend to have larger enrollment but that, too, is not always the case.

LIBERAL ARTS COLLEGE. A liberal arts college is one that focuses on the breadth of education and teaching students critical thinking skills. Their emphasis is largely focused on problem-solving ability, and you will often find writing and public speaking woven throughout the curriculum. Liberal arts colleges can be public or private.

PRIVATE COLLEGE. Private institutions are funded by tuition as well as private donors and are not supplemented by tax dollars. Private schools can be religiously affiliated, but some are without ties to a specific religion. While the sticker price is usually higher on private institutions, if a student receives significant scholarships then it can drastically reduce the cost of attendance.

Now that you have a clearer understanding of what the TYPES of postsecondary options are, complete the wish list (parent and student) to get an idea of what characteristics you each may want from the college experience. You will find your Wish List Questionnaire at the end of this chapter. Once you have your wish list(s) completed, use the information to answer questions on a college search site. There are several you can use through Princeton Review, Big Future, etc. (See a list of college search sites in the websites section at the back of this book.) Once you have input your criteria, the site will produce a list of colleges that fit your wish list.

You can then begin your initial research on colleges from this list and determine if the colleges you are looking at do indeed demonstrate a potential fit for you. As you learn more about different schools, change your mind, and learn more about yourself, then you can simply input new criteria and generate another list of colleges. This isn't a one-and-done approach. This is an ongoing, evolutional process that requires research and trial-and-error. Giving yourself enough time to dream, investigate, and change your mind takes a lot of pressure off. Trying to cram this all in at the end of junior or into senior year is only going to cause angst. Start dreaming in the beginning or middle of your sophomore year and just have fun with it. By the time you get to your junior and senior year, you will find your list of schools will be coming together nicely and you'll have a better sense of what you're after in a college.

I'd like to add advice when it comes to creating your wish lists and tentative list of schools to start researching and visiting. First, this process will always be about compromise. Parents and students often disagree in the beginning about what they want in a school. I encourage you to be open to discussing your viewpoints and listening to one another. You and your parents will both favor schools that the other doesn't agree with. Compromise, and go on visits for each other's sake. If you like a school that they don't care for, and vice versa, handle the issue fairly: visit both schools. That way, you and your parents both have a chance to see what you're rejecting.

The point here is that no one really knows the right answer when they start the college search process, but it's important to be open to each other's viewpoints and see for yourself if it is a good fit. Letting go of preconceived notions as well as not following the crowd is key. Choose your battles.

Oftentimes, the process of applying to college takes care of itself. I have seen many a family have a battle in my office when a student says they want to go to California from the Midwest and the parents argue it's too far. I always encourage them to add the school to the list and not make every school that far away so they don't have all their eggs in one basket. That's compromise. It also buys some time for the application process to sort itself out over time. In the end, one of a few things usually happens: The student doesn't get in, the student decides after a period of time it's too far away, the financial aid doesn't come through and the family can't afford it, or the parents visit and fall in love with it. Regardless, don't try to win the battle at the expense of losing the war. When you get down to it, everyone wants the same thing. And that same thing is a good FIT for the student where he or she can be productive, successful, and happy.

ACTION STEPS
for Chapter 6

FIGURING OUT WHAT YOU WANT

1) Educate yourself on what the various options related to college are (public vs. private, 2-year vs. 4-year, etc.).

2) Have both parent and student take the wish list questionnaire on the next page.

3) Fill in each person's answers on the grid to see where there are agreements and differences and discuss where there might be compromise.

4) Construct a list of potential colleges using the information on your wish lists and enter it in a college search program such as www.bigfuture.com or using your school's college search program. (Check the website listing at the back of this book for a list of college search sites.)

5) Based on the results you get, you can start to do research on schools and gather more information to see what schools might be worthy of a campus visit.

WORKSHEETS FOR CHAPTER 6

COLLEGE WISH LIST QUESTIONNAIRE

DIRECTIONS: Each deciding member of the family (parent(s), student, etc.) should answer the following questions independently and without input from the other members as it relates to the high school student and what is viewed as "best fit" for the student. Once everyone has completed the questionnaire, put all the answers onto the tri-column answer sheet and look for commonality and discuss differences. This will help you discern where there is consensus and where there needs to be compromise. From here, a potential list of colleges can be created by using college search websites such as Big Future or Princeton Review.

CIRCLE THE ANSWER(S) THAT ARE MOST APPEALING TO YOU FOR EACH QUESTION:

1. Level of School: TRADE SCHOOL 2-YEAR 4-YEAR GAP YEAR MILITARY

2. Type of School: PUBLIC PRIVATE DOES NOT MATTER

3. School Gender(s): CO-ED SINGLE SEX

4. Religious affiliation school should have (optional):_____

5. Community Size: RURAL SMALL TOWN LARGE TOWN SMALL CITY LARGE CITY

6. Where to live: ON-CAMPUS HOUSING COMMUTE

7. Size of School: Under 2,000 2-5K 5K-10K 10K-15K 15K-20K >20K

8. States considered: _____

_____

9. Driving distance from home: < 2 hrs 2-3 hrs 4-6 hrs 7-8 hrs >8 hrs

10. Major(s) school should have (up to 3): _____

_____

11. Sport that will be played competitively (if applicable): _____

    11a. At what level? NCAA Div I NCAA Div II NCAA Div III NAIA

12. Other important criteria school must have (ROTC, Greek Life, support for those with

learning differences, etc): _____

WISH LIST RESPONSES

QUESTION	STUDENT	PARENT "A"	PARENT "B"
1. Level of School (2-yr / 4-yr / Trade)			
2. Type of School (Public / Private / Doesn't Matter)			
3. Gender of School (All Male/ All Female/Co-Ed)			
4. Religious Affiliation (n/a if public schools only)			
5. Community Size			
6. Where to Live (on campus or commute)			
7. Size of School			
8. States Considered			
9. Driving Distance			
10. Major(s)			
11. Sports/Level (athletes only)			
12. Other criteria (Study Abroad / Greek Life / Intramurals / Etc.)			

CHAPTER 7

Step 2: Standardized Admission Testing

············ **TIMELINE:** ············

**JUNIOR YEAR (PREFERABLY SECOND SEMESTER)
THROUGH 1ST SEMESTER SENIOR YEAR**

Standardized testing is one of those things that throw people off for a couple of reasons. First, let's face it. Testing can be boring. Schools do so much testing of their own that students are ready to blow off whatever college entrance tests they need. Unfortunately, standardized testing is a necessary evil in most (but not all) cases. Your test scores affect not only your admission chances but scholarship chances as well. Colleges and universities require standardized testing because it is a simple, uniform way for them to put every applicant from all over the country on the same scale. Curriculum, grading scales, and rigor varies greatly from school to school. Standardized testing allows colleges to have everyone take the exact same test and see how they do.

There is a lot of debate these days about standardized testing and its worth. I'm not here to debate its worth or fairness. I am here to give you the facts about when it is a good idea to take the tests and what your other options might be if you are not a good test taker. Once you understand the options available to you, you will be able to make a good decision about which test (or tests) are right for you. I will also touch on some standardized tests available for students earlier in high school that will prepare them for the real college entrance exams. Regardless, remember this section is to give you the BASICS about college admissions testing. It will not address all scenarios and all needs for everyone reading this book. Always enlist the help of your school's counselor, college admission representative, or additional reading sources on this topic.

ENTRANCE EXAMS REQUIRED BY COLLEGES

Let's start by talking about what the standardized test options are. There are two mainstream college admission tests that colleges and universities use. One is the ACT (American College Testing), and the other is the SAT (Scholastic Aptitude Test). These are two different companies in two different parts of the country who offer a testing service. ACT is located in Iowa and has historically been the test of choice for colleges in the Midwest and the central portion of the United States. The SAT is located in New Jersey and has long been the test of choice for the upper echelon schools and the coast schools.

In years past, colleges and universities would require one test or the other and students would have to register for the tests according to which schools they were interested in applying for admission. Now, however, since we have become such a mobile society and so many schools are clamoring for applicants, that rule of thumb has lessened, and things are starting to muddle a bit. In many cases, a college or university will accept either test (with no bias or preference), and students have the freedom to take the test that benefits them the most. It is your responsibility, however, to find out which tests the schools will accept. You will find this by checking the schools' websites for admission requirements or enlisting the help of the school's admission representative.

THE DIFFERENCE BETWEEN ACT AND SAT

What is the difference between the two tests? ACT has four sections to the test (English, math, reading, and science) with an optional writing section students can register to take. The score range for the ACT is 1-36. (It's important to note here that the score is not as revealing as the percentile associated with a score. The percentile is what tells you how you scored in relation to others. If you don't understand percentiles, ask your counselor to explain your test results to you.)

The ACT relies heavily on knowledge of learned material the student has been exposed to in the classroom. When you (the student) register for the ACT, you will automatically take the four above-mentioned sections the day of the test. Whether you register and take the writing portion is up to you. Writing is required for some schools' admissions process, but not most. I usually advise students to NOT take the writing portion on their first go at testing just because it adds stress and length to the test, not to mention cost. I do advise students to take it at least once, though, so that if they find a school that requires the writing portion for admission, they are covered.

The SAT, on the other hand, relies not only on what the student has learned but some deductive reasoning. There are two sections of the SAT: Critical Reasoning (English) and Mathematics. The score range for the SAT is 400-1600. (Remember, to put into context how you did on the test, you need to understand percentiles because that is what gauges how well you did in comparison to others.) The SAT also had a required writing section for some time, but recently disbanded that part of the test. Most students who have taken both the ACT and SAT will often find they do better on one test or the other. The key is to find the test that is best suited for you and which one is needed for admission to the schools you are interested in attending. I still find that which tests students take are geographically influenced (Midwest students gravitate to the ACT and the coast students to the SAT).

HOW TO DECIDE WHICH TEST TO TAKE

The best way to decide which standardized test to take is to take pre-tests (or practice tests) in both the ACT and SAT to determine what your predicted scores might be for when you take the real deal. ACT has offered several tests over the years that have a predictive quality in determining what a student might get on their ACT. These tests have gone under several names—P-ACT, PLAN and ASPIRE. This test is usually offered during the sophomore year within the school day. (Students will often have to sign up to take the test so pay attention to any information that is sent to you regarding testing.) The pre-test is set up just like the real ACT but is geared for sophomores regarding content. The results of this pre-test will give a current score, but also predict a score range (and percentiles) for the actual ACT.

This information is extremely helpful to counselors when working with a student to identify potential colleges. It allows the counselor to have an idea of what the student's score might be and can help him or her start to identify potential schools that may be a fit long before the student takes an ACT. If your high school doesn't offer these pre-ACT tests as a sophomore, ask if they offer a practice ACT. A practice ACT is an actual ACT test (like the one given to juniors and seniors for admission), but it is given to students during the school day (or on a weekend) under the same test conditions as a national ACT test. The results of this test are not sent to colleges, but give students an opportunity to see how they do, and it also gives them a score that will serve as a baseline and help them have an idea of what score range they might get when they take the ACT 'for real.'

SAT offers a similar system of pre-testing known as the PSAT (The "P" stands for "preliminary"). The test dates are set nationally each year, and it is offered on two different days in October of the student's junior year (a Wednesday and a Saturday). While it is not uncommon for a sophomore to register for the PSAT, the test is geared for students with a junior level of learning so the test can most accurately predict SAT score ranges when the student takes the test in the junior year.

Keep in mind, the PSAT has a program called the National Merit Scholarship Qualifying Test (NMSQT). When students take their PSAT in the fall of their junior year, they are automatically eligible for the National Merit competition. This program awards recognition and scholarships to high achieving test takers on the PSAT. The score needed to qualify as a National Merit Semi-Finalist or Finalist is determined by each state as they award to the top percentages of their individual state's highest scorers. Students who are National Merit Semi-Finalists or Finalists can win scholarship money from either National Merit directly or a corporation which sponsors a National Merit Scholarship program. Additionally, some colleges offer large (sometimes full-ride) scholarships to National Merit semi-finalists and/ or finalists to attend their campuses. They do this to draw smart students to their campus and, also, who wouldn't want to brag and say we have "X" number of National Merit semi-finalists or finalists on our campus? Most students are not going to be National Merit semi-finalists or finalists, and that's ok. Usually, about the top one-half of the top one percent of all testers within a given state earns the distinction of finalist. That's a pretty narrow group. The reason I bring it to your attention, though, is to remind you to do your personal best on the test because it can bring monetary rewards if you end up doing well. If you are a home-schooled student, contact the nearest high school to ask to be included in the PSAT testing during the junior year. While you will have to pay the fee required to take the PSAT, most schools will accommodate you if possible.

So how does taking a "pre" SAT or ACT help the student? First, since the pre-tests are fashioned in the same format as the actual SAT or ACT, it gives a student the opportunity to get a feel for what testing will be like. Secondly, because the pre-tests give predicted scores, it will help students know what their score range will be on the actual entrance tests and it will help them know if they need to focus their energy on one test or the other, or if they'd like to try taking both. Be sure to find out when pre-tests are offered early on in high school. Once you miss these test dates, you often cannot take them at another time.

HOW TO REGISTER FOR AN ACT OR SAT

When the time comes to register for the actual ACT or SAT, you will need to go to the testing agency's site to register. To register for the ACT, go to their website (www.act.org) and follow the registration links. Create an account with your demographic information and then select a test date. (They are always held on Saturdays.) One piece of information you will be asked to provide is your high school code (also called a CEEB code). Your high school code is a six-digit code assigned to your specific high school. You will want to provide this information so your high school has a record of you taking the test. You will be able to find the CEEB code on the website as a search option or you can usually find it on your high school's website or counseling page. In addition to your high school code, you will be choosing a test center as well. Most students choose their own high school as a test center or one where they will be near that weekend. (You can register for any test center in any state for a national test date so if you are traveling for vacation or sports, you can still test.) You will also be asked if you would like any colleges to receive your test scores (you can send to up to four schools for free anytime before the actual test date). After your test date, you can still send scores to colleges but will then have to pay a fee. You will also be asked a series of other questions regarding your test results, and then you will pay by credit card on the site. The ACT is offered several times per year, but remember that registration for a given date often closes almost six weeks before the actual test date. All test dates and deadlines are listed on the site for you to reference.

The process for SAT registration is similar to registering for the ACT. Go to www.collegeboard.com to register for this test. Once on the site, look for the link to register and follow the directions. The only difference you will likely see is there is no choice on registering for the writing portion of the test since SAT no longer offers it. Remember, deadlines happen long before the test date so be sure to register early. Also, you will have to provide a photo ID so be prepared for that.

TEST PREPARATION FOR ACT AND SAT

Prepping for the ACT and/or SAT by doing some review work is a great way to try and improve your score. If you want to do some review, there are several ways to do this. The first would be to check with your high school (or a neighboring high school) to see if they will be offering some sort of review class. There may or may not be a charge for this class based on how the school handles fees. This usually offers students a fairly affordable way to do prep for the test in a class setting. These classes are usually offered after school or on weekends prior to a specific test date. Students might also consider doing a one-on-one review for a specific portion of the test (Math, English, etc.). There are tutors out there who do one-to-one work with students. They might help you review for a specific subject or test-taking strategies as a whole. Ask your counselor for some recommendations. Lastly, students may want to purchase a review book. You can buy these online from Amazon or at your local bookstore (go to the educational testing section). There is also a great deal of information online at both ACT's and SAT's websites so students can review electronically through their individual sites or find resources they partner with to help you review. If you google 'ACT or SAT review' you will find several options. In addition to SAT and ACT's own websites, you can also use other programs like Princeton Review. Most online options are free. If you are interested in learning more about pre-testing for either SAT or ACT, check with your counselor and they will tell you which tests they offer and when.

RE-TESTING MULTIPLE TIMES

One of the most frequent test-related questions I get asked by students is if they can take their ACT or SAT repeatedly to try and increase their score. The answer is YES! Currently, the ACT is offered six times per year (February, April, June, September, October, December) and the SAT is offered seven times per year (January, March, May, June, October, November, December). In 2018, there are plans to add additional summer dates to the testing schedule. This gives students ample opportunities to test repeatedly to improve their scores. You will notice, too, that the two different types of tests are sometimes offered in the same month. However, the dates are staggered, so you won't have to choose between one test or the other on the same date. You can always find information on the test dates for each year on each of the test's websites.

WHEN TO TEST FOR THE FIRST TIME

I advise students to take the test the second semester of the junior year. Many parents want to start their students in the sophomore year with the ACT and SAT. Their rationale is that the more opportunity to practice, the better they will score over time. While that rationale may initially appear sound, the reality is that the test is based on what the student has learned. So, if you test a student in the sophomore year, they often will not have learned enough of the material on the test until various points in junior year, so they often leave frustrated and discouraged. If you keep testing the student over and over, by the time they get to the fall of their senior year when they should be hitting their stride, they've either stopped testing or given up. Starting too early can backfire.

A more productive use of test time might be to take the pre-tests in the student's sophomore (PLAN or ASPIRE) or junior year (PSAT) to help them see what their predicted scores might be. My advice? Leave the ACT and SAT to junior and senior year. However, every student's situation is different, and you have the prerogative to begin testing at any time you see fit. If you have been enrolled in multiple advanced or honors courses and are a great test taker and feel comfortable taking the test sophomore year or early in junior year, then go for it! You may be ahead of the curve in your learning and ready sooner rather than later. Again, when to test is ultimately the decision of each individual family.

NUMBER OF TIMES TO TAKE ENTRANCE TESTS

How many times to take a college entrance exam depends on the student and their needs and goals. I would say the average number of times my students take the test is about three. Most students I've talked with will take it more than once. Doing this takes pressure off the student for a 'one and done' experience. They know that if they are going to test repeatedly, they don't have all their proverbial eggs in one basket. One approach might be to take the test once as a baseline with no practice, then, on the second attempt, do some test prep in advance of the test. By the third attempt, you should be working to master your score. Often you will start to see a pattern in your scores over time. When you start seeing the same score over and over, it may be a clue to stop testing as you may have reached your testing potential.

WHEN TO TAKE YOUR LAST ENTRANCE EXAM

When to stop testing again depends on your situation. I would say if you've taken some pre-tests and you know what your predicted score is for ACT and/or SAT and you are hitting that top predicted score, you may be capping out on your high score. If you want to try and beat that, keep testing. If not, call it done. Keep in mind, however, to do your homework with admissions and scholarships. If you are missing a scholarship cutoff by a small margin, ask the school what is the last test date you can try to get that score. You may find they tell you December (or even up to June) of your senior year. If that's the case and you want the money, you may want to keep testing to get that extra point. As far as admission goes, you probably want to have testing for that wrapped up by December of your senior year. Every school has different deadlines for this, so be sure to ask each college you are looking at what their policy is.

WHAT WILL HAPPEN IF YOU RE-TEST AND GET A LOWER SCORE

Colleges give students the benefit of the doubt and want them to succeed. They understand some tests go better than others and they aren't out to sabotage you. Schools will take the highest composite score even if there's a lower one. I have talked to many a college representative over the years, and they have always assured me they want to give students every chance to succeed, and they will always take the highest score on a standardized test assuming it is taken within the normal timeframe required to submit scores for admission. Because colleges take a holistic approach to applications and look at several deciding factors when considering an admission decision, testing is just one part of it.

Again, schools want you to succeed. In fact, some schools do what's called "super scoring" when it comes to the ACT or SAT. What they do is they take the HIGHEST subject area score from each test you've submitted to them, and then creates a higher overall composite score. So, let's say you got a lower composite (overall) score on your April ACT, but your English and Reading scores were higher on that test than your June test. A college that super scores would take your English and Reading scores from your April test and your Math and Science scores from your June test and create a new, higher ACT composite score that will benefit you for both admission and scholarship! Therefore, there can actually be a benefit to taking the test multiple times and sending those scores to the colleges! Not every school super scores, so ask your admission representative what the policy is for their school.

SENDING SCORES TO COLLEGES

Each time you register for testing, you will be given the option to send a handful of scores for free to the colleges of your choice. To do this, you will choose up to four colleges you would like to receive your scores. When prompted, you will do a search for the school (make sure you have the right campus) and enter their four-digit code. This will allow the testing agency to send your scores for this specific test date to the schools you have chosen. You don't have to send your scores out sight unseen, but many students choose this option. It is important to note that many don't do it the first time they test because they don't know where they want to apply just yet. If you want to see what your score is first and then send them to schools, that is fine. Just don't forget to do it! I have seen students go through the whole admission process only to be denied because they forgot to send their scores and so their applications were considered incomplete!

An official copy of your scores must be sent directly from the testing agency (ACT or SAT) to each college you are applying to. If you choose to send scores AFTER you've taken the test, there is a fee to send each test score for a given date to each school you want to receive it. If you request scores to be sent at the time you register for the test, you can usually send to four schools for free. If you want to save the money and send your scores as you go, there is no problem with that strategy either since schools will take the highest composite score you send them when considering you for admission and scholarship. However, remember you will be sending your scores sight unseen since you requested they be sent BEFORE you even took the test, so you don't know the actual scores.

I want to acknowledge that there are parents and students out there who are protective and private about sending scores to colleges and only want to send their one BEST test results. I get that. But for most folks in most situations, sending multiple scores is not an issue. Deciding what scores to send is a personal one and you need to decide for yourself if you should send scores from multiple test dates as you go along or just the best one at the time you submit your application. This decision is personal and financial for most people. Do what is right for YOU. But don't forget to send your BEST score! If you apply in October and send a score only to get a higher score in December, ask the school if they will take your December test score. If the school still will take your December score, make sure it gets there! Your higher score may help you be admitted or yield more scholarship money from the university.

WHAT TO DO IF YOU DON'T TEST WELL

In the event you are not a good test taker, do not lose hope! There are currently about 800 schools nationwide that have become known as "Test Optional" schools. They understand that there is more to a student than their test scores. These schools have opted to take a more holistic approach to looking at a student's file, and so your application (and interview) will have to be very strong. They will consider other aspects, such as GPA, course rigor, school involvement, interviews, and essays and will determine if they feel the student will be able to succeed at their institution without ever looking at an ACT or SAT score! Please note, however, that if you do send scores to these schools, they will become part of your file and used to make admission decisions. If you don't want your test score to be a part of the admission decision at a test-optional school, don't send it to them! If you would like a comprehensive list of schools that are currently test-optional, go to www.fairtest.org to search the database of schools and learn more. Even if you are considering applying to a test-optional school, you should still consider taking your standardized admission test at least once, so you have it if needed in the event you decide to apply to a non-test optional school.

ACTION STEPS
for Chapter 7

STANDARDIZED ADMISSION TESTING

1) If you are an underclassman, consider taking a pre-SAT or pre-ACT test through your high school to get a predicted score for SAT and/or ACT.

2) Register during the second semester of junior year for ACT and/or SAT. (ACT: www.act.org. SAT: www.collegeboard.com.)

3) Research and pursue test preparation programs (classes, books, tutors, etc.).

4) Re-test as needed on subsequent dates throughout junior and into senior year.

5) If you are not a good test taker, research your options with Test Optional colleges at www.fairtest.org.

CHAPTER 8

Step 3:
Visiting Colleges

························ **TIMELINE:** ························

SPRING SEMESTER OF JUNIOR YEAR - SPRING SEMESTER OF SENIOR YEAR

(Summer after sophomore year for local colleges to get a baseline)

Visiting is the best part of the whole college process! It is not only fun getting to see the possibilities come to life, but **visiting is the number one way students make a decision about where they want to attend college.** Once a student gets to the campus and can see themselves as part of the community and its programs; it gives them momentum for the rest of the application process. The problem I see with visiting is that most people just get in the car and go with no thought as to what they want in a college, and run blindly from place to place. However, if you made a good effort creating your wish list, you are in great shape. Hopefully, talking as a family about what characteristics you want in a school and from the college experience gave focus to what schools are worthy of a visit from you.

I want to add a caution about creating a list of schools to visit. Often, when I suggest a college that is checking off all the boxes on their wish lists, families will say to me "Well, I've never heard of that school." Just because you've never heard of a school, doesn't mean it isn't a great place. They are approximately 5,000 post-secondary schools in the United States. I've been doing this for over 20 years, and I don't know them all! The only way you are going to know if a school is a great fit for a student is to see it for yourself!

The best way to start the college visiting process is in your own backyard. While I tell people to start their official process of visiting colleges by the second semester of their junior year, why not start close to home the summer between sophomore and junior year and even the first semester of junior year? Here is an example of what I mean:

In the Midwestern city where I live, we are blessed to have an abundance of colleges and universities that fit a wide range of criteria---big, small, public, private, elite, liberal arts, etc. You name it, you can get to it within a 2-hour drive. "Well, I don't want to attend school in this city and/or state" is a common response I get from students. My response to them is that no one is trying to make you stay close to home, but looking at what is close by provides a compare-and-contrast situation for what you do and don't want. Visit schools early in the search process that fit a wide range of criteria and see if you do want a small school (or a big one). Do you want to be in a city or in a rural community? Because you've never spent much time on college campuses, you need to SEE and EXPERIENCE something to get a baseline of what you do and do not want. It's sort of like dating for schools. You need to see what's out there before you commit. Doing this will also help you amend your wish list as you gather more information about what you do want from your future school and allow you to focus on schools that fit the bill.

My suggestion is to look at schools within a two or three-hour radius from your home beginning in your sophomore year of high school. Get a feel for what you are attracted to based on these initial visits and make a list of those qualities. Then, expand your search to include a wider swath of real estate and go out 200, 300, 400 miles or whatever distance you are comfortable with traveling. Look at schools that fit your criteria and set up more visits. Taking this approach can help you streamline your process and narrow down an otherwise extensive list of schools. You might also consider doing what's called a preview day. Many colleges offer preview days (open houses) for sophomores as well as juniors. These events can give you a great overview of what the college offers. You will want to do individual tours and appointments at a later date for those schools still in the running.

Remember, to make a list of your qualities, use your wish list criteria from Chapter 6. It is designed to be revisited and reworked as you move along throughout the process and change your mind about what you want. Identifying characteristics such as distance from home, size of school, type of school, major, etc. will all help focus your search. To find a complete list of schools that fit your criteria, you have two options. The first is to utilize a college search software program your school may have. Ask your counselor if there is such a program your high school uses to help students search electronically for colleges. If not, consider free online searches. One of my favorites is Big Future available through the Collegeboard website.

You can also enlist the help of an experienced college counselor by utilizing your student's high school college counselor (which is free to you). Or, you can hire a private college counselor to help you. (On a side note, if you go the private college counselor route, be sure to ask LOTS of questions about their training, experience, and the like. Anyone can say they are a college counselor as credentialing is loosely defined.) In either case, use the items from your wish list to determine what characteristics you want in a potential college. Once you've entered those characteristics, the software will generate a list of schools for you to consider. Or, if you're utilizing a human, he or she can also suggest schools that might be a fit based on what you think you want. (It is common for humans to utilize online search aids as well, so don't be surprised if they do.)

Once you have identified some schools that you would like to visit, you will need to contact them to set up that visit. For them to help you once you are there, they will need to know in advance what exactly it is you would like to see and accomplish while you are on campus. I always tell families I work with that if you want to get an accurate feel for a college make sure you look in every nook and cranny. Beyond the usual tour, the prospective student may want to sit in on a class to make sure they are challenged enough (or not over-challenged). They will probably also want to see a dorm, eat the cafeteria food, talk to professors about a specific major they are interested in, and get a feel for what the social aspect of college might provide (sporting events, concerts, clubs, etc.). As for parents, they are most often concerned about financial aid, campus security, etc. It is not unusual for a family to take a 'divide and conquer' approach while on a visit. While the student heads off to observe a class, the parent may meet with the financial aid office or seek out answers to other questions they may have. If you tell them when you call exactly what you want to accomplish while you are there, the admissions office can set up everything for you so your visit is productive. If you just "drop in," chances are you will not be met with a warm welcome in the midst of their busy schedules. Remember, my hope here is to EMPOWER students, so I have included three forms at the end of this chapter that will help the student to set up their visits:

1) A form that walks the student through how to set up a college campus visit via EMAIL

2) A form that walks the student through what to say and request when CALLING to set up a visit

3) A detailed list of questions students might want to ask when visiting each campus

Additionally, here are a few more tips on visiting colleges. First, **try your best to visit when school is in session.** It gives you a clearer picture of what college life is like on a typical day. Not all schools have classes on Fridays, for example. Or, don't schedule a visit only to find out the school is on spring break while you are there. A lot of people tell me the only time they can visit colleges is in the summer when their schedules are less hectic. I completely get that. There is nothing wrong with that, but if you like what you see on a summer visit, I encourage you to take a second visit when school is in full swing. Schools are way more than just the campus and buildings. It's important you see the people who will be around you each day as well and get a vibe of the campus energy.

The idea of visiting when school is in session naturally leads to the question "What if I CAN'T visit? The school is too far away for us to get to at this early stage." That is a common problem many people face. Let's say you live somewhere on the east coast and you are considering a university in California. Not exactly down the street, right? What many people will do is stay in good contact with the admissions representative assigned to them and build a relationship with them via email and phone. They might also meet with the representative when they are in the student's community so they can connect a name to a face. Some schools utilize their alums in various cities to meet with the prospective student and interview them and report their findings back to the admission office. Regardless, stay connected with the university and its people! Then when you ARE admitted, and the school is still a strong contender, splurge and buy your ticket to get out there and visit. Don't handle all your schools this way though. You will need to visit as many of your schools as possible early on, so you make sure you are barking up the right tree and finding schools that are a good fit for you.

Secondly, **make an official visit through the admissions office.** Students sometimes just head off to a college for the weekend and visit with a friend they know who goes there and say they 'visited.' The friend shows them around and takes them to the fun parties. The admissions office has no idea the prospective student is even on campus! The problem with this is that there is SO much information the admissions office provides that a current student cannot. Also, some admissions offices track prospective student interest. If a student has visited the friend ten times and the admission office has no idea, they may think the student has no interest in attending when the truth is they are interested! The admissions office needs to know their prospective students so they can advocate for them in the admission and scholarship process. They can't do that if they don't know you! If you can't visit, you can demonstrate your interest in other ways by visiting with the admission rep when they are in town or visiting your high school or by sending an email or making a call to them. Whatever you do, don't think more is better. They may track your interest, but a million emails get a little annoying, and that tactic may backfire on you!

Also, **try to spend the night in the dorms if possible.** Most schools have ambassador programs that set prospective students up with their best representatives in the student body. They can answer questions, show them around, and give them an up-close-and-personal look at the school. Many students I know opt to spend the night with someone they know who goes to the school. The problem with this is it sways the student one way or the other and doesn't necessarily give an objective picture of what college life is like there. Often, students have a false sense of security because they know the person. What is most impressive is the situation where the student likes the school not knowing anyone there beforehand and yet still feels comfortable there.

Lastly, **write down your impressions after every campus visit.** Make a list of pros and cons. What did you like or not like? Were there any red flags? What was your overall vibe of the place? If you are going to visit several campuses, eventually it all starts to run together. Write things down immediately on the way home from your visit, and you will have a much more accurate picture that will provide you with good information. I've put a College Visit Log worksheet at the end of this chapter to help you keep track of your impressions of each college visit.

Visiting is a lot of "Lather, Rinse, Repeat." It is a lot of repetition. You'll probably get sick of doing it after a while, but I cannot stress the importance enough. And, the good news is, the more you do college visits, the better you will get at figuring out what you like and don't like! Over the years, I have had students just pick up and go to a college sight unseen. In most cases, they transfer after just a semester. Do your due diligence and visit, visit, visit!

Once you've completed your visits, you will need to decide which schools are worthy of an application from you. Do not put all your eggs in one basket when it comes to admission. I've put a worksheet at the end of this chapter to help you strategize your list of schools. You ultimately want to apply to 1 or 2 schools in the "Reach" category.

That is, you don't know if you can get in or if you can afford it. We call this the dream school. The second tier is for the "Probable" schools—I can get in here, I think we can afford it, and I'd be happy here. (Pay attention to this section because this is where many students end up!) You should have 2-3 of these schools. Lastly, have 1-2 back-up schools in case you need a fallback. Remember, spread things out financially, academically, and geographically! This will give you more options and guarantee success. If you have questions about your strategy and selection of schools, enlist the help of a counselor who can help you know your admission and financial aid chances.

ACTION STEPS
for Chapter 8

VISITING COLLEGES

1) Use your 'wish list' items from Chapter 6 and use an online search program utilized by your high school, a free search site, or personal resource (counselor) to help you create a master list of potential schools.

2) If you don't know what you want in a school (big, small, etc.), visit a variety of schools within a 2 or 3-hour radius of your home to create a baseline of what you like.

3) Once you have a clearer picture of what qualities you like in a school, use your resources (online or human) to create a list of potential schools that fit those criteria.

4) To set up a visit, use the handouts included in this chapter to help you set up a productive visit as well as know what questions to ask when you are on campus.

5) Using the College Visit Log at the end of this chapter, write down your impressions of each school after your visit including likes, dislikes, red flags, etc.

6) Visit, visit, visit! It is the #1 way students choose their school.

WORKSHEETS FOR CHAPTER 8

SAMPLE EMAIL FORMAT TO SET UP A COLLEGE VISIT

Begin your email with an introduction of yourself including what city and state you live in as well as what high school you attend. The body of your email should express interest in WHEN you would like to visit campus as well as WHAT you (and your parents) would like to see and do while you are there. (This is wide open---meet people such as professors in your major, admission reps, financial aid officers or see things like counseling centers, campus security, etc. It is up to YOU.) The closing of your email should ask for any contact information you would like for the admission representative as well as thanking them for their time to help you schedule your visit.

HERE IS A SAMPLE OF WHAT YOUR EMAIL MIGHT LOOK LIKE:

Hello! My name is _____ and I attend _____
                                                        (Name of High School)

in _____ . I am interested in setting up a college visit for
        (City and State)

_____ on _____
        (Name of College)   (Day/Date/Time)

In addition to having a formal tour of the campus while I am there, I would also like to

_____ and _____
(Sit in on a class, talk to a professor, see a dorm, etc.)

My _____ will also be with me that day and they would like to
        (mom/dad/parents)

_____ if possible. Can you help us arrange this?
(List who they'd like to talk with, things to see)

Lastly, may I please have the name and contact information for the admission representative assigned to my school in the event I have any questions?
Thank you for your time! I look forward to hearing from you.

Sincerely,

_____ (Your Full Name Here)

SAMPLE DIALOGUE TO CALL AND SET UP A COLLEGE VISIT

CALL THE UNDERGRADUATE ADMISSIONS OFFICE AT THE SCHOOL OF YOUR CHOICE. YOUR DIALOGUE SHOULD FOLLOW ACCORDINGLY:

INTRODUCTION:

"Hello. My name is _____ and I'm calling from _____."

(City/State)

"I'd like to speak with the admission rep/visit coordinator who works with

students from _____ in _____."

(High School)   (City/State)

BODY:

ONCE YOU ARE TRANSFERRED, RE-INTRODUCE YOURSELF AND THEN TELL THEM:

"Hi. I am interested in setting up a college visit for _____ .

(Name of College)

and we plan to be in the area on_____."

(Day/Date)

"We would like to have a tour of the campus that day and while we are there, I (student) would like to do the following (sit in on a class, meet a professor in my major, see a dorm, etc.):

_____"

(A few things **you** would like to do while on campus)

"My (mom/dad) will also be attending and they would like to (visit with someone from Financial Aid, Student Services, Counseling, Campus Security, etc.):

_____"

(A few things **your parent(s)** would like to do while on campus)

"Can you help us arrange that as well for the day we are there?"

CLOSING:

Thank you for your help. Lastly, may I please have the contact information (name, email, phone) for my admission rep while I have you on the phone?

"Thanks again. We look forward to coming."

> **TIP**
> *The more information you can give to the admissions office regarding your visit and what you want to accomplish while you are there, the more successful your visit will be.*

QUESTIONS TO ASK ADMISSION REPS

ABOUT ADMISSIONS

What is the deadline to apply for admission?

Do you require the SAT or ACT? Do you require any additional testing?

Do you require the writing section of the ACT?

What do you look for in a student who wants to attend your school?

How can I increase my chances for admission?

What can I do to get my foot in the door at your school?

Does it help me in the admission process if my ___ (Parent/Brother/Grandma) went here?

Do you have a study abroad program? Are costs included in my tuition? Where can I go?

ABOUT SCHOLARSHIPS

What are the academic/testing requirements for freshman scholarships?

What is the deadline to apply for scholarships at your school?

What is the 'ballpark average' for a scholarship package each year?

How can I increase my chance of earning a scholarship?

Are there departmental scholarships available for my major?

Is there a separate scholarship I need to complete to receive merit aid?

Do you allow me to bring in private scholarship money and 'stack' it on top of other scholarships you've given me?

Regarding institutional scholarships, grants or other resources, be sure to ask if the award is a one-year award or renewable for all four.

ABOUT ACADEMICS

What support do you give freshmen to get acclimated and stay on track academically?

Do teachers' assistants (graduate students) teach classes or full professors?

How big is the largest class for a freshman intro class? An upper-level class?

Do you have a writing center available if I need help?

What kind of tutoring is available and in what subjects?

How much time do students typically spend on homework each day/week?

Is there an opportunity to do research as an undergraduate?

Do you have an honors college?

QUESTIONS TO ASK ADMISSION REPS

ABOUT SETTING UP VISITS

When is a good time to visit and look around campus?

How do I go about setting up a visit?

Can I meet with professors or talk to other campus personnel while I am there?

Do you do weekend visits?

ABOUT LIVING ON CAMPUS

How are dorms set up? (suite style, apartments, etc.)

If I decide to enroll, when are housing applications due?

Can I bring a car to campus the first year?

What percentage of students live ON campus?

Am I required to live in a campus dorm as a freshman? Sophomore?

I love to eat! What are the dining options? Are the dining halls open every day?

Tell me about the surrounding community where the school is located.

What is transportation like to _____ ? (your hometown)

How close are you to airport, bus, or train?

Do you give any discount for transportation? (buses, subway, trains, etc.)

ABOUT SOCIAL LIFE

What types of entertainment (comedians, concerts, play productions) come to campus?

Do students get discount (or free!) tickets to sporting events or concerts?

What activities go on near or on campus? Clubs, events, etc.

Do students hang around on the weekends or go home?

What is there to get involved in/do on the weekends?

How do you help students get to know one another?

ABOUT GETTING INVOLVED

I want to get involved in _____ (intramurals, theater, volunteer, etc.).
Do you have this available on your campus? If so, how can I get involved?

Do you have a recreation center?

I want to be involved with (theater, music, etc.) but don't plan to major in it. Can I still participate in these activities as a non-major?

Do you have a Greek system? When does rush for sororities and fraternities happen? If I don't join a fraternity/sorority my freshman year, can I do it in a later year? What percentage of campus belongs to Greek life? Does Greek life have its own housing?

ABOUT MAJORS AND CAREER SERVICES

What are your most popular majors?

I want to major in _____. Are there any specific admission requirements or deadlines to be admitted to that particular program?

Am I guaranteed my major upon admission to the university? (direct entry)

Tell me about co-op, internship, or research opportunities related to my major.

I don't know what major I want! How do you help students like me figure it out?

I want to major in _____. Can you tell me if I can get into this major as a freshman?

I'd like to know more about internships and co-ops to help me work in my field. Do you offer these? If so, how many and in what majors?

Do you have a Career Services office? What things will they do to help me find a job, write a resume, or figure out my major?

How are internships set up?

What percentage of students complete an internship?

Can you provide examples of internships in my field of interest?

What percentage of your students secure a job or get into graduate/professional school within six months of graduation? Of that number, what percentage of students responded to the survey or request for information?

What percentage of your graduates have jobs within six months of graduation as compared to enrolling in graduate school?

ABOUT THE NUMBERS

What percentage of students come back from freshman to sophomore year?

What percentage of your students graduate in four years?

I'm interested in _____ (medical school, law school, etc.) after college. How many students from your college apply to these schools after they graduate and how many get into these graduate programs?

ABOUT ATHLETICS

What percentage of athletes graduate in 4 years?

What is the academic policy regarding athletes missing classes due to competitions?

What type of academic support (tutors, study groups, etc.) exist for athletes?

QUESTIONS TO ASK ADMISSION REPS

ABOUT SPECIALIZED LEARNING

Are there any programs in place to help students who have learning disabilities or need a tutor?

What level of support is offered for students with learning differences? (A comprehensive support program or just extra help such as tutoring, extended time, etc.?)

Who provides support? (professional staff, graduate students, undergraduate students, etc.)

If a comprehensive program exists, what is the ratio of professional staff-to-students in the program?

Is there an extra cost for the program? If so, how much per semester?

Can you opt-out of the comprehensive program at a later date (after freshman year)?

Does support exist in the formal sense after freshman year? Elaborate.

Is there a separate application form or process to be considered for a comprehensive program?

What documentation do we need to provide to be approved for accommodations?

ABOUT OTHER RANDOM QUESTIONS TO ASK CURRENT STUDENTS

What would you like to tell me about your school that I've not asked?

What do you like most/least about your school?

What would you change about your school?

What made you choose this school?

Where else did you apply?

What do you wish you knew as a freshman that you know now?

What advice would you give me?

What is a typical day like for you on campus?

ABOUT "DEEP QUESTIONS" TO ASK FACULTY

What distinguishes an outstanding student on your campus?

What does success/happiness look like here?

Where can I take ownership here?

Where can I take advantage of opportunities?

Complete this log after each visit to a college. Record your impressions immediately after your visit so you don't forget the impressions from your visit. Doing this will help schools from running together and give you an accurate picture of your experience.

COLLEGE	LIKES	DISLIKES (RED FLAGS)	"GUT" FEELING	CONTENDER? (YES / NO / MAYBE)
Example: ABC College Anywhere, KS	• Good internship opp. • Like dorms and food • Good nursing program • Qualify for scholarship • Has Greek Life	• Feels a bit big • Rec center needs update • Nursing program is not direct entry	• Overall 'good' vibe / can see me here • Students and faculty are nice • Good energy on campus • Room to grow • Overwhelmed by size of campus • Concerned about getting in nursing	Yes

COLLEGE VISIT LOG

COLLEGE	LIKES	DISLIKES (RED FLAGS)	"GUT" FEELING	CONTENDER? (YES / NO / MAYBE)

COLLEGE VISIT LOG

COLLEGE	LIKES	DISLIKES (RED FLAGS)	"GUT" FEELING	CONTENDER? (YES / NO / MAYBE)

COLLEGE VISIT LOG

COLLEGE	LIKES	DISLIKES (RED FLAGS)	"GUT" FEELING	CONTENDER? (YES / NO / MAYBE)

HOW TO CREATE A LIST OF SCHOOLS
WHEN DECIDING WHERE TO APPLY

You never want all your eggs in one basket. When deciding where to apply, do your homework to research admission statistics, test scores, fit, etc. beforehand. Then parent(s) and student need to have a lengthy discussion about what schools seem to be a good fit for each of the following scenarios. Then, create a list of about **FIVE to SEVEN** schools that include:

REACH SCHOOLS

Choose **1 or 2** schools that fit this description: "Not sure if I can get in or afford it, but if the stars aligned in my favor, this is where I would love to be." (AKA: the 'dream school')

1. _____ .

2. _____ .

PROBABLE

Choose **2 or 3** schools that fit this description: "I can do this! I like these schools! I can see myself going here and being happy. I am fairly certain I can get in, and it is likely financially doable." (Many students end up at one of these institutions, so choose wisely!)

1. _____ .

2. _____ .

3. _____ .

THE BACK-UP PLAN

Choose **1 or 2** schools that fit this description: "If all else fails, I will go here. It covers me in case I need to be close to home, in-state, or have an affordable option in the event I would have a major financial setback or if family or personal circumstances dictated. It wouldn't be my dream, but would be better than not going to school at all." (This assures you have all your bases covered no matter what happens.)

1. _____ .

2. _____ .

NOTE: You need to have one school minimum in each category with heavy emphasis on the probable category. Once you have an agreed upon list, these are the schools to which you should apply.

CHAPTER 9

Step 4:
Applying for Admission

.... **TIMELINE:** ....
AUGUST OF SENIOR YEAR – DECEMBER OF SENIOR YEAR
(Note: This timeline will fluctuate some depending upon deadlines
for each school.)

Aside from paying for college, the actual process of applying to college is probably the most cumbersome part of the college process. The biggest help in simplifying the application process is three-fold:

1. UNDERSTAND THE TIMELINES UNDER WHICH YOU MUST WORK. Unlike the random classroom assignment for which you may have been able to navigate an extension, college admissions (and the financial aid and scholarship process) are largely unforgiving. It's not their concern that you have been busy with school, sports, or otherwise. It's your job to get things in on time or risk the consequences; this usually means missing out.

To better facilitate the process of deadlines (and help with organization), there is an application checklist grid at the end of this chapter that, when completed, helps students to see at a glance what schools they are applying to, what documents are required to complete the application and the deadline for applying. To begin, write down the name of each school you (the student) will be applying to and then fill in the additional information as research is completed.

2. GET YOURSELF ORGANIZED. This means getting a binder, expandable folder or other office supply product that works for you. In this, you can organize everything you need for the process including keeping track of passwords, timelines, business cards or other contact information, and any paperwork relevant to the schools or other information you have been given. Remember, any worksheets within this book are designed to be cut out and hole-punched and placed in your binder for easy reference.

3. SET ASIDE TIME TO WORK ON APPLICATIONS. Applications can be a complex to-do list depending upon what documents are needed to make the application complete. In addition to completing the application online, students may also need to provide a resume or student activity list, essay, submit test scores and transcripts, letters of recommendation, and pay an application fee. Ideally, students should set aside a small block of time each evening when they do their homework to work on their applications. Adding in 20 minutes each evening to your homework time to put together an activity list or fill out an online application will make a big dent in the process and make it a LOT more manageable. If that schedule doesn't work, try scheduling firm blocks of time (be consistent) when you can work on things. For example, every Sunday from 1-4pm. The more realistic and consistent you are with a timeframe that works for you, the more successful you will be in completing things on time. It's no different than scheduling homework time or practice time for sports. If you treat completing your college applications like a class that requires homework, you'll schedule time for it in your day just like any other class.

Once you feel that you are organized and have set aside planned time to work on college applications, you need to also understand the three different types of admission deadlines: **rolling admission, early action,** and **early decision**. It is important that you understand the differences in each of the options because they each come with different sets of timelines and rules.

The first of these is **rolling admission** and is how the majority of schools operate. In a rolling admission process, a student applies and the admission office will process the application when it comes in and then notify the student of the admission decision. That's not to say there aren't special circumstances for rolling admissions. For example, there may be earlier application deadlines for a student to meet to qualify and be considered for scholarships. So, if a school operates under rolling admission, the student can generally apply and be accepted at any time. However, if the student waits until the second semester of senior year to apply and there is no scholarship money left, the student may gain admission but not have any scholarship money to offset the cost of attendance.

Under **early action,** students who apply by an earlier deadline than the regular applicant pool deadline will be notified at an earlier date. In this example, the school's regular admission deadline may be January 1 and the student will be notified of the admission decision by mid-February (or as late as April). Early action candidates might have a deadline of November 1 (two months earlier) and may have a decision on their admission by the end of December. The advantage for an early action applicant is that colleges sometimes pick a larger amount of the pool from the early action pool than they do from the regular decision pool that comes in later. This makes sense for the colleges to do this because they are essentially picking the cream of the crop in the first round. For the student, if the college is high on the list and they want to potentially increase their odds for admission, it makes sense to file early action. If not, you can wait for the regular decision pile. Some schools are Single-Choice Early Action (also called Restrictive Early Action) meaning you can only apply to ONE school as an early action applicant. Students applying to a college with a Single-Choice Early Action program cannot apply to other schools as an early action applicant. If you are applying under early action, you can apply to as many schools early action as you would like. If you are admitted from the early action round (Single-Choice or Early Action), you are NOT obligated to attend the school if you are admitted.

Early decision is a whole different animal. Early decision candidates follow much of the same procedure as early action candidates do--they apply in and are notified of admission in an earlier timeframe than the regular pool. The biggest difference is that if a student is admitted to a college under early decision, they are obligated to attend that university once admission has been granted. When a student applies early decision, he or she must sign a contract as part of the application process that is signed by the student, parents, and school counselor indicating the student understands the obligation that, if admitted, he or she must withdraw all other applications and must enroll in the school. This is a huge commitment.

Essentially, the student must decide to attend this university once the application goes in assuming admission is granted. There is consideration for financial need and admission offices will collaborate with the families to work out those details in advance of an admission decision, so the family knows what their merit or aid package may look like. If you make the decision to break your early decision contract and think you will just enroll elsewhere, it may be a problem for you. If another school you try to attend knows of your contract breach, the potential is there that your admission at your alternate school may be jeopardized. I cannot stress the importance of taking an early decision contract seriously. Because you are under contract, you may NOT apply to more than one school as an early decision candidate.

I do not advise early decision for most students. There are a few exceptions where I have seen it work well. The first is an athlete who is committed or signed with a university's athletic program and needs to be admitted academically. The second is a student whose family has decided that they are 100% committed to a school and know they will not, under any circumstances, change their minds. And, last is a student whose parents work at the university, knows the bill is paid for, and that specific school is his or her number one choice. Beyond that, I find early decision premature for students who are not ready to make a commitment as early as December of their senior year. Early decision is not just 'seeing if I can get in.' It is **a binding contract** that can have legal consequences if broken.

Once you have determined the admission deadline you will use, determine HOW you will apply to each school. While most if not all seniors apply online, there are a few colleges that will still accept paper applications. To be truthful, I've not handled a paper application in over a decade. Electronic is the way to go. There are several ways to apply to college including the Common Application, Universal Application, Coalition Application and application via each school's own website. The first three listed allow you to apply to various schools through one application. However, there are two major application platforms that are most popular currently.

The first is the Common Application. The Common App is accepted at about 700 of the 5,000 institutions in the country. The schools on this list are primarily private institutions, but there is a growing list of public institutions that will now accept the Common App. The advantage to the Common App is that you only fill out your demographics and other application materials (including the essay) ONE time. From there, you send the application to whichever schools accept the Common App that you would like to receive your application for admission. (Please note that some schools will require supplemental materials in addition to the Common Application itself so be sure you are giving the college the information they require.) Some schools that accept the Common App also waive the application fee, making it a cost-effective option. You can go to the Common App's website at www.commonapp.org and search the college list to see if the specific college(s) you are interested in accepts the Common App. If a college does not accept the

Common App, you will then have to go to the school's individual website and click on the Admissions tab and follow the instructions there to submit your application and other required credentials. The best way to determine your course of action is to first check the Common App website and see how many of the schools you are planning to apply to accept the Common App. The more you find, the better the news for you because you will fill out one application for submission to numerous schools. Whatever schools do not take the Common App will likely default to the second popular application platform which is the student applying via the schools' individual websites. There you will either apply directly to the school via their website or they will direct you to another application platform to complete your application.

For schools that accept both the Common Application as well as have their own application, students will often ask me "which one do colleges prefer and does it matter in the admission process?" The short answer is "either one" and "no." Colleges who accept the Common App as well as have their own application have no preference and give equal credence to either one. Whatever you do, **do NOT fill out both!** You create a logistical nightmare for the admissions office when you do this!

To keep track of which college accepts what type of application, use the application checklist grid on the following pages to help you get organized. First, list the schools you are applying to at the top of the columns provided. After you do this, go to the Common App website and do a search for each of your schools. When you are on the site look for a tab that reads "Explore Colleges." Make sure you have the school's name spelled correctly. If the school's name pops up in the search, they accept the Common App. Once you find your school, click on the "Add to My Colleges" button. (You will not be able to do this until you open an account for yourself.) This will add this institution to your dashboard, and you can then work on the application and ultimately send it to each of the schools on your dashboard. You can always take a school off your dashboard later if you decide not to apply. Once you've hit submit on your application to send it to a given school, however, there is no changing your mind.

To find a list of what the list of requirements are to apply to each school (essay, letters of recommendation, etc.) click on each of the schools you have added to your dashboard. At the top of your dashboard, you will see a tab marked "My Colleges." Click on it, and you will see a section of required materials to make your application complete. Read through the section to determine what is needed, and then transfer your information to your grid. (You can also find the Requirements Grid on the Common App site and download it for ALL schools' requirements.) Putting your information on the grid will allow you to easily see deadlines, fees, the number of letters of recommendation and essays required. This will help you stay organized and on top of things. Put the grid at the front of whatever notebook, binder, or folder you use to organize yourself for the college process. It will provide an easy visual for you to keep track of things. Applicants are responsible for knowing and providing (on time) the materials needed for admission. **While colleges might be courteous at times in pointing out what is still missing from the file, it is ultimately the student's responsibility to complete the application in a timely fashion to be considered for admission.**

Once you have determined which colleges will take the Common App, move on to the other schools on your list. To determine what they need for admission, you will go to each school's individual website. The Admissions tab is usually front and center on each school's site. Follow it, look for a list of requirements needed for admission, and record it on your grid. If you've searched high and low for information and can't find a specific piece, contact the school (or your rep) and ask them.

When your grid is completed, you will have a sense of order to things and be able to start working on the specific pieces that will go into making your application complete. Below is a list of things that MAY be required of you in the admission process and some tips on how you should go about completing each piece. Remember, your admission process may involve the help of teachers and counselors, so you want to give them enough time to complete things for you.

1. **THE APPLICATION.** Applications themselves are not particularly hard to complete. Most of it is demographic information like addresses, birth date, parental information, and courses taken. You will find the repetition of inputting information tedious, though, and that's why the Common App can be handy because you will only fill out the demographic information once and it can be sent to multiple schools. Applications can ask for detailed information about parents' educational pasts including where and

when they attended college and what degree they attained. If your application requires this information, you will likely need to get this information from your parents. (If you are using the Common App, they do require this information.)

2. ESSAY. The essay is often the most challenging part of the application. Not all schools require an essay for admission. Many larger public institutions, for example, do not require essays while many private and/or smaller schools will. The essay required for schools on the Common App has a word requirement of 250-650 words. I would follow this length requirement for all schools not on the Common Application unless their directions state otherwise. Remember that your essay is only one piece of your application. The essay is important, though, because it gives you the opportunity to share with colleges who you are as a person and they can see how you might fit at their college. Essays are designed to be a creative outlet and an expression of who you are and what makes you tick.

One of the most impressive examples I have of a great student essay came from a college application workshop I was teaching. I was talking with my students about being creative with their essays, and one student was clearly stuck. I encouraged her to take a break and that eventually, an idea would come to her. Later in the class, she was talking with a friend who asked her if she'd seen the most recent episode of a popular TV show. She responded saying she had not because she didn't have a TV set in her home. Instantly, I turned to her and said, "There's your essay!" It was a unique aspect of her life most couldn't relate to or had not experienced. From there, she developed a fabulous essay detailing the many ways she spent her time by not spending it watching TV. She explained to the admission committee her love for theater and acting and how this was her entertainment. She also explained her love for conversation with others and ability to live in the moment and not be subject to advertisements or other outside influences. Her admission process went smoothly, and more than one college rep commented to me on her unique essay.

My advice? Find the mundane in your life and find the value in it. This is where the good stuff happens. One tip I often give students is to work backward on your essay. Decide first what you want the admission committee to know about you and then decide which question to answer. This way you don't get hung up on the question since you already know what you want to convey. I give a detailed example of working backward to create your essay as well as other suggestions for writing your essay in the Tips for Writing Your College Essay worksheet at the end of this chapter. Whatever you do, FOLLOW THE DIRECTIONS! If a college asks you to write on a specific topic or question, oblige them. You may write a great essay on a certain subject, but if it's not the topic they want to hear about, all you're doing is showing that you can't follow directions.

3. LETTERS OF RECOMMENDATION. Letters give teachers the opportunity to tell schools about your specific strengths and attributes you will bring to the college. Choose your teachers carefully. Make sure they like you! (Just because you did well in a class doesn't mean the teacher will write you a good recommendation.) **It is important that you give them a minimum of 2-3 weeks to write your letter.** It is important to ask in person first if they can write the letter followed by detailed written instructions on what you need including deadlines. Look for a sample format letter for requesting letters at the end of this chapter that you can follow to make your own letter of recommendation requests if your high school does not have its own form. Always follow your school's policy on requesting letters of recommendation and transcripts. Just a quick word here on who you choose to write your letters. Students tend to ask the person whose class they sailed through with no struggles or difficulty. I will tell you, in my own experience, that sometimes the teacher whose class you struggled in the most is the BEST writer of your letter. He or she can explain to the admission committee your work ethic, problem-solving ability, and tenacity. This sometimes speaks volumes more than the class in which you were the star and got the easy A. Also, remember letter writers are never "required" to write you a letter of recommendation. If someone is kind enough to write a letter on your behalf, be sure to send them a thank you note.

Lastly, it is common for the application to ask you (the student) to choose whether you waive your right to see your application and its supporting documents. This includes your letters of recommendation. You are free to answer the question either way. Keep in mind, though, that when a school sees you've waived (given up) your right to see your letters written by your teachers, they feel your letter writers are free to be exceptionally honest. Your letter writers are people you choose, so you should feel safe in giving up your right to see your application file and know they will do a wonderful job advocating for you. In all my years of being a counselor, I have had very few students not waive their rights to their file. Most waived their rights and trusted the process. However, you should choose whatever option with which you are most comfortable. Keep in mind, though, if you don't waive your right you can only see your file to the school to which you were admitted and enrolled assuming their policy is to keep your application file. So, you don't really have that much free access even if you don't waive your right.

4. TRANSCRIPTS. A transcript is the official record of your demographic and educational information from a given school. In addition to your identifying information such as name and address, it also lists each course you have taken, final grade, and credit awarded. Also listed is attendance and GPA. In some cases, some high schools' transcripts also include standardized test scores. Beware, however, that most colleges do NOT accept standardized test scores (ACT and SAT) as official when listed on the student's transcript. You will have to have your scores sent directly from the testing agency. Most colleges will require your transcript be sent at the time you submit your application. When looking at your transcript, colleges will examine several things including GPA and the rigor of your courses. Did you take all 'blow-off' courses or did you challenge yourself with a tough course in a subject or two? In most cases, colleges like to see a challenging course with a bit lower grade than 'fluff' classes where you got an A but didn't learn much. The transcript gives the college a quick snapshot of your academic journey. You will need to request your high school transcript from your counselor or registrar's office. Give them about two weeks' notice to process your request. It is important you remember they process a LOT of transcript requests, so you may have to 'get in line' and wait your turn. Waiting until the last minute to request a transcript (or a letter of recommendation) will never work in your favor! If you have a deadline to make for your application to be complete, this includes RECEIVING your transcript. As an example, if your deadline is December 1, you best have made your transcript request by November 15. This should give your counselor or registrar adequate time to fulfill your request by the December 1 deadline. To make your request, you will either go online to your school's request system or fill out a paper request. Ask your school counselor how to do this if they've not already given you instructions. Make sure you are familiar with your school's deadline policy for requesting transcripts.

5. ACTIVITY LIST. An activity list or resume is not always required to complete your application. However, it is a nice touch to your application file. While the Common Application and some other schools give you the space to list your top 10-12 activities, providing them with your own custom-crafted activity list demonstrates initiative, interest, and professionalism. Always list your most prominent activities on your activity list and always list your most important one first. **Quality always trumps quantity when it comes to an activity list.** A laundry list of activities is never as impressive as your dedication to a few important activities where you've demonstrated passion and the opportunity to grow. For example, it is better that you have only 4 or 5 key activities that demonstrate longevity and commitment to an activity (all four years on the swimming team), leadership (team captain) and progression (improvement in records or qualifying for state) over being involved in 15 clubs you may or may not have attended a meeting for or may have only participated in for a year. We call that longevity and increased roles and responsibilities 'depth' and colleges love to see depth in activities. It demonstrates passion and commitment.

When you make your activity list, be sure to also add those activities not directly related to school but still demonstrate commitment and give a clear picture of what your life looks like. Think part-time jobs, theater productions not related to your school, church youth groups, scouting, volunteer service, or recreational teams. It all counts and provides examples of your ability to multitask and be well-rounded. Ideally, students should be keeping track of their activities from their first day of freshman year. (No college is interested in any activity earlier than 9th grade unless you managed to win a Grammy or Academy Award, let's say. Otherwise, 9th grade is your starting block. If you go back farther than that, it looks like you're trying to stretch to come up with something.) To help you brainstorm your list of activities you might want to include on your activities list, you can use the worksheet at the end of this chapter. The worksheet is designed to help you categorize your activities (academics, athletics, leadership, volunteer service, miscellaneous, etc.). You can decide your own headings depending upon your interests. If you've spent a lot of time in robotics, research, or music, you might want to make a category just for those activities. Don't feel you must use any category headings other than those that showcase your activities.

Once you have listed your activities on the worksheet, type up the information into a logical and easy-to-follow presentation in either a resume or activity list (grid-style) format. (I've included a sample of both a resume and an activity list at the end of this chapter so you have a visual.) The most important aspect of any activity list or resume is the DESCRIPTION section. It is not enough to say you were part of the Spanish Club, an admission rep needs to understand YOUR contribution to your activity. As an example,

STEP 4: APPLYING FOR ADMISSION

if you list soccer as one of your activities, it is also important to note your personal details such as position played, statistics or records, awards, and so on. If you are part of National Honor Society, it is not enough to be a member. Admission reps need to understand what you did to contribute to the group. Listing things like what service you did as part of the club and leadership positions you held within the club give them a clearer picture of your role. If your club is unique to your school, you might also have to explain what the purpose of the club is. Listing yourself as a member of the "Game Club" tells the reader nothing. Is it for board games, video games, or otherwise? A brief explanation of the club's purpose might be necessary to educate the admission rep as to what the club or organization's purpose is if it is not a widely-known activity such as National Honor Society, Thespian Club, or soccer.

In addition, your activity list or resume should include your identifying information including your name, date of birth, and high school at the top of each page. Again, while an activity list or resume is rarely required, it is a nice touch to make your file stand out and gives you the opportunity to highlight your accomplishments over the last four years. I had one university tell me that while 90% of all their applicants did not submit a resume or activity list, those who did were more likely to make it to the advanced scholarship round. This may bode well for you as taking the time to put more effort into your application may pay off financially. Whatever you do, be truthful. Lying on anything you submit as part of the application process is justification for having your admission revoked if you are caught. If a college determines you have lied on any aspect of your application, they will rescind your offer of admission even if you've already been accepted.

The convenient thing about creating your own activity list is that you can use it repeatedly for many schools so long as it follows any format stipulations they may have. If you can, upload a pdf version of your activity list directly to your application online. If that is not an option, I suggest you send a pdf version of your activity list electronically to the admission representative assigned to your high school and ask him or her to add it to your file. Sending it in a pdf version is important because it will hold the formatting for the reader on the receiving end. There would be nothing worse than if you put a lot of effort into making your activity list or resume look nice only to have it arrive unreadable or misaligned when the recipient opens the attachment. Again, a resume or activity list is not a requirement but ALWAYS a nice touch. Remember, a job worth doing is a job worth doing well! You will never get a second chance to make a first impression.

Giving the college information about what you've done (and ultimately who you are as a person) is key in helping them about making an informed decision about admitting you to their school. However, in addition to (or sometimes in place of) the written activity list or resume outlined above, some students are opting to go high tech. As an example, ZeeMee (www.zeemee.com) is one online platform that allows students to upload videos and images that highlight their accomplishments and activities. It gives another dimension to let colleges see who you are as a person and not just facts on a piece of paper. Students send their electronic file link to the college so admissions can watch their clip. Most videos are less than two minutes long. If you're interested in seeing sample ZeeMee videos, you can do a search on YouTube.

I read admission applications for a major university each year and, at this point, I only see a handful of video clip files each application season. However, as our younger society becomes even more tech savvy, I think we will see an increase in information being submitted to colleges in video and image format versus paper and will see more options as far as companies that will provide these types of services. The most important aspect is that the student gets the information about themselves to the colleges, and it probably doesn't make a huge difference if they do it electronically or in paper format.

Once you have gathered all the pieces necessary to submit your complete application (application, essay, letters of recommendation, transcript, activity list, test scores), you will need to submit all these pieces for your application to be complete, and keep in mind that each piece is rarely sent together at the same time. Your high school will send your transcripts and letters of recommendation as you request them. You will submit your application, essay and activity list. Additionally, YOU will request your test scores be sent directly from the testing agency. ALL these pieces need to reach the school by the designated deadline. So, if your college's deadline is December 1, my recommendation is that you have everything timed out to arrive by the end of November at the latest. Because your process involves other people (teachers, counselors, testing agencies), you must let them know what you need from them a MINIMUM of two weeks prior to the deadline. (In this case, November 15). This gives them adequate time to do what you need them to do. Check your high school's and the testing agency's policies. You may find they have different deadlines than the two-week one outlined above.

Once you have your applications submitted, you will usually receive one of two decisions: accepted or denied. You might also find yourself on a **waitlist** which means you have not secured a spot in the freshman class, but may if space becomes available. If your #1 school waitlists you, you might want to contact them with any changes regarding GPA, activities, etc. as well as express the fact their school is your #1 choice. This will let them know you are serious about enrolling and could possibly move you up the waitlist. Always talk to your rep!

I think it's also important to acknowledge here that your pecking order of where you want to go may change after you apply and that is normal. Your number one school in August may not be your number one by December or in April prior to the May 1 decision deadline as you move through the admission and financial aid process. I've put a worksheet at the end of this chapter so you can track your pecking order of schools as you move through senior year.

ACTION STEPS
for Chapter 9

APPLYING FOR ADMISSION

1) Understand timelines and deadlines for individual schools.

2) Set a specific time each day/week to work on applications.

3) Keep track of all your important website addresses, log-ins, and passwords on the Password Log worksheet (end of this chapter) as well as your admission rep contacts on the Contact Log (at the end of Chapter 5).

4) Decide HOW you will apply to schools (Common Application versus the school's individual application or another application platform).

5) Complete the application grid for each school's requirements and refer to it to keep yourself on track.

6) Write admission essay (if required).

7) Secure writers for letters of recommendation (if they are required).

8) Request high school transcript be sent to EACH of the schools to which you have applied.

9) Request standardized test scores (ACT and/or SAT) be sent to each of the schools to which you have applied.

10) Create an activity list using the worksheet provided and then type it up into resume or activity list format. Send it to each of the schools to which you have applied.

11) Once you are admitted to a university, be sure to read all the paperwork they send you including housing contract information which may have important deadlines. You don't want to miss out on housing options. There is still a lot of paperwork to do once you've been admitted!

WORKSHEETS FOR CHAPTER 9

COLLEGE APPLICATION CHECKLIST

COLLEGE	ABC University			
ACCEPTS COMMON APPLICATION?	YES			
APPLICATION DEADLINE	December 1			
APPLICATION FEE	$50.00			
# OF REC LETTERS NEEDED	1			
# OF ESSAYS REQUIRED	1			
ACTIVITY LIST/ RESUME NEEDED?	YES			
MID-YEAR REPORT? (C. A. ONLY)	YES			
TRANSCRIPT NEEDED?	YES			
TESTS REQUIRED (ACT OR SAT)	ACT			
IS THERE A SEPARATE SCHOLARSHIP APP TO BE COMPLETED?	NO			

COLLEGE APPLICATION CHECKLIST

COLLEGE	ACCEPTS COMMON APPLICATION?	APPLICATION DEADLINE	APPLICATION FEE	# OF REC LETTERS NEEDED	# OF ESSAYS REQUIRED	ACTIVITY LIST/ RESUME NEEDED?	MID-YEAR REPORT? (C. A. ONLY)	TRANSCRIPT NEEDED?	TESTS REQUIRED (ACT OR SAT)	IS THERE A SEPARATE SCHOLARSHIP APP TO BE COMPLETED?

Use the log below to keep track of all your websites, user names, and passwords. Many students try to use the same format for user names and passwords, but many sites require different formats. Listing your information here will keep everything in one place so you don't have to request your passwords every time you try to log in.

EXAMPLE			
WEBSITE	**WEBSITE ADDRESS**	**USERNAME**	**PASSWORD**
Common Application	www.commonapp.org	johndoe@aol.com	Gamer123

APPLICATIONS			
WEBSITE	**WEBSITE ADDRESS**	**USERNAME**	**PASSWORD**

PASSWORD LOG

STANDARDIZED TESTING			
WEBSITE	WEBSITE ADDRESS	USERNAME	PASSWORD

OTHER			
WEBSITE	WEBSITE ADDRESS	USERNAME	PASSWORD

TIPS FOR WRITING YOUR COLLEGE ESSAY

THE COLLEGE ADMISSION ESSAY IS DESIGNED TO:

- Help the admissions committee get to know you better
- See you as a person and understand what makes you unique
- Allow you to tell them more about you that was not obvious in other parts of your application
- Give more information that might make them go to bat for you in the admission process
- Encourage you to provide an understanding of how you might fit in their student body

A TYPICAL, BORING, OR BAD ESSAY MIGHT INCLUDE THESE TOPICS:

- The volunteer service project
- The overcome sports injury
- One that has no enthusiasm
- One that makes it seem like you are trying to give the 'right answer'
- One that is 'factual' but not interesting

A GOOD OR INTERESTING ESSAY MIGHT INCLUDE:

- Humor
- Examples of overcoming obstacles
- One that is compelling to read
- Talks about hobbies or talents
- One that tells a story
- An opening sentence that grabs the reader's attention
- One that paints a picture of the situation you are trying to convey
- One that is just about your everyday life and what makes you happy, passionate, and/or moved to action

TIPS TO BRAINSTORM ESSAY TOPICS:

- Keep a notebook (or your phone) handy to record ideas that pop in your head.
- Have someone ask you a potential essay question out loud and then try to answer it. This may get rid of writer's block.
- Pick something quirky or mundane and build off that.
- Sum up your life in a six-word sentence and then expand on it. This will help you focus on a specific point of information you'd like to make. ("Farming is always in my blood.")
- Brainstorm adjectives that describe you. Set a timer for 30-seconds and jot down all the adjectives that describe you. Afterward, look at the list to see if it produces any ideas.
- Free association – Set the timer for two minutes and write whatever comes to mind!
- Think about your major. Was there a hobby that led to your interest in that?

- Consider using analogies.
- Decide what you want them to know about you and THEN choose the question to answer (see example below on working backward).

POSSIBLE TOPIC STARTER QUESTIONS:

- What is the most significant experience in your life?
- What is one characteristic of yourself that is so YOU, you couldn't be you without it?
- What is the biggest lesson you've ever learned?
- What is the funniest thing that's ever happened to you? What did you gain/learn as a result?
- Who has impacted your life the most—personally, academically, athletically, spiritually, etc.?
- What is your best memory from childhood?
- What are you most passionate about in life?
- How would your parents/grandparents/siblings/friends/teachers/coaches, etc. describe you?
- What is your biggest failure? What did you learn from the experience?
- What is your dream for your life?
- How do you react to setbacks?
- Name a unique or quirky thing (or two) about you and/or your life.
- What makes you gloriously happy?
- What would cause you to speak up?
- What bugs you?
- What's your average Friday, Saturday, Sunday, Monday...like?
- What are some routines or habits you have?
- What is one boring or ordinary fact about your life?
- Name one thing you can't live without.
- What's your biggest regret?
- What would you tell your future self?
- What's the ONE thing you want the admission committee to know about you?

TIPS FOR WRITING YOUR COLLEGE ESSAY

TIPS FOR PRODUCING YOUR BEST ESSAY:

- Always have someone proofread your work for the mechanics—grammar, spelling, etc.
- Always have someone give creative feedback—does it hold the reader's interest? Does it make the reader know you better?
- Make sure you respect the word count maximum. If you don't, the end of your essay will be cut off mid-sentence!
- The mundane can be stunning when re-framed into a clever observation or analogy.
- Don't wait until the last minute to craft your essay.
- Don't try too hard. Just be yourself.
- Remember that the essay is only one segment of the total package that is your application!

WORK BACKWARDS TO ANSWER THE ESSAY QUESTION

The example below is one I use with my students all the time. Think first of what you want the admission committee to know about you and THEN choose the question to answer. In other words, know what you want to say and then find the question that best allows you to do this. One of the best answers I have ever heard using this example is this:

Student wants the admission committee to know: How important her family is to her.

The question she chose to answer based on the topics the college gave her to write about: What is the best invention ever? (This seems like an impossible question to answer based on what she wants them to know!)

Her answer: The kitchen table.

There was no mention of technology, cell phones, computers, or any other gadget someone might typically respond when asked this question about best inventions. She chose a simple piece of wood with four legs as the greatest invention. From there, she conveyed that the kitchen table was the greatest invention because this is where she and her family gathered each night to share their day, share a meal, and tell their stories. It was a place where memories were made. Had she looked at the list of questions FIRST and then decided to answer, she would've come up with a much more traditional and canned answer that didn't tell her story. By knowing what she wanted to tell them about herself, she could then make the question fit her answer. There is no "right" answer to any essay question! That's the secret. It's just how you spin your story. It seems backward (and it is), but it works fabulously and makes for a unique, clever, personal, and memorable essay!

HOW TO CREATE AN ACTIVITY LIST

1) List your activities by **category.** (Honors/Awards, Athletics, Employment, Service, School Clubs, Leadership positions, Activities Outside of School (Scouts, etc.), or any other category you can think of that you will need to tell them about your involvement and/or accomplishments. Use as many (or few) categories as you need to accurately convey yourself.

2) List the **position** you held or **position** you played, etc. within that activity along with the **year(s) of participation.**

3) In the **Description** category, list YOUR contribution to the activity. This description allows you to explain to the admissions committee what you did and accomplished.

NOTE: Activity lists can be formatted in many ways. This is only an example to list your activities before you begin the construction of your list. Display your information in the manner that best reflects you.

CATEGORY:

ACTIVITY	POSITION	9	10	11	12	DESCRIPTION

CATEGORY:

ACTIVITY	POSITION	9	10	11	12	DESCRIPTION

CATEGORY:

ACTIVITY	POSITION	9	10	11	12	DESCRIPTION

HOW TO CREATE AN ACTIVITY LIST

CATEGORY:

ACTIVITY	POSITION	9	10	11	12	DESCRIPTION

CATEGORY:

ACTIVITY	POSITION	9	10	11	12	DESCRIPTION

CATEGORY:

ACTIVITY	POSITION				DESCRIPTION
	9	10	11	12	

CATEGORY:

ACTIVITY	POSITION				DESCRIPTION
	9	10	11	12	

John Q. Public
Anytown High School
DOB: 01/01/2002

ACTIVITIES

NATIONAL HONOR SOCIETY   11, 12
- Attend meetings regularly
- Participate in service projects including soup kitchen volunteer and tutoring math
- Elected vice president of club for senior year

SPANISH CLUB   9, 10, 11, 12
- Attend monthly meetings at school
- Participate in cultural exchange events within community
- Assist in planning and executing of Cinco de Mayo celebration

THESPIAN CLUB
- Work as ticket seller for upcoming theater events
- Attend speaker presentations by actors from area theater community
- Served as secretary of club during junior year

SERVICE CLUB   9, 10, 11, 12
Volunteer at area charities including:
- Our City Homeless Shelter
- Annual Thanksgiving Dinner event
- Children's Hospital clerical worker
- American Red Cross blood drive

ATHLETICS

SOCCER   9, 10
- Played Junior Varsity for Anytown High School
- Goalie and defender positions
- Voted Most Improved Player after freshman year

MISCELLANEOUS

MCDONALD'S RESTAURANT   11, 12
- Crew member
- Greet customers and take orders
- Clean dining area and take out trash
- Perform other duties as assigned by manager

BOY SCOUTS   9, 10
- Attended meetings regularly
- Camp leader for group
- Participated in various service projects including tree planting and park clean-up

SAMPLE ACTIVITY LIST

Jane Q. Doe
Anywhere High School
DOB: 02/02/2002

HONORS AND AWARDS	DESCRIPTION	YEARS PARTICIPATED
Student of the Month	Awarded to student demonstrating superior in academics and character	9
Outstanding Science Student	Chosen by science faculty and given to student who demonstrates strong interest in biological sciences and lab work	10
Perfect Attendance Award	Recognized at Spring awards ceremony for no missed school days	9, 10, 11
Most Improved Actor	Awarded by theater department for improvements in technique	11
Girl Scout Gold Award	Previously earned Girl Scout Silver Award and completed additional 80 hours of service	12

THEATER	DESCRIPTION	YEARS PARTICIPATED
Prop Crew	Worked behind scenes for fall play; attended all play practices	9
Sound Crew	Responsible for assisting sound board for spring musical including mics/special effects sounds	9
Chorus Member	Sang in Chorus for spring musical "Annie"	9
Actress	Walk-on part for fall play "Into the Woods"	10
Actress	Actress in "Death of a Salesman"	11
Actress	Lead actress 'Sandy' in spring musical "Grease"	11

SAMPLE ACTIVITY LIST

Jane Q. Doe
Anywhere High School
DOB: 02/02/2002

VOLUNTEER SERVICE	DESCRIPTION	YEARS PARTICIPATED
American Red Cross	Phone bank volunteer for annual fundraiser	9, 10
Our Town Soup Kitchen	Serve weekly meals for homeless year-round	10, 11, 12
Children's Hospital	Volunteer reader to kids during story time (1 hr/week – summer months)	9, 10, 11

OTHER ACTIVITIES	DESCRIPTION	YEARS PARTICIPATED
Lifeguard for Swim Club	Certified lifeguard (including CPR); worked appx. 20 hrs/week	9, 10
Girl Scouts	Active member including fundraising, community service, and attending weekly meetings	10, 11, 12
Our Town Church Youth Group	Participated in church-sponsored activities including retreats, volunteer work, and monthly social activities	9
Dance	Took classes in ballet, tap, and jazz on a weekly basis. Performed in bi-annual recitals.	9, 10, 11
Foreign Exchange Program	Studied abroad the second semester of junior year and lived with host family in France	11
Babysitting	Work for several families doing babysitting on as-needed basis	9, 10, 11, 12

REQUESTING A LETTER OF RECOMMENDATION

1) Ask the individual IN PERSON first to see if they are willing to help you. If they say yes, provide them with the following information (either electronically or on paper—whatever format the recommender would like or your high school's policy dictates.)

2) Using the sample below, choose which components below you want to include in your personalized version of this form letter. (Make sure your school doesn't have a request form already in place that you are required to use.) Type your custom letter and give/send to your recommender.

3) Give the individual 2-3 weeks to complete your letter. (Make his or her deadline earlier than the application deadline in case he/she forgets.) Ideally, you will ask the individual in the fall of senior year unless your school's policy and timeline are different.

3) Write the individual a thank you note once the letter has been composed and submitted.

Date: _____
      (Fill in date you give teacher this request)

Dear _____ .
      (Teacher/counselor name)

Thank you for agreeing to write a letter of recommendation for me as part of my college application process. The deadline for you to submit my letter of recommendation is:

_____ .
      (Day and date)

Please submit my letter to: _____ .
      (Electronically or hard copy to counselor, Common App, mail directly)

Here is some information and background about me that may be helpful to you in writing my letter:

My full name is: _____ .
      (Official name on school records)

You taught me in _____ during my
      (Subject/s)

_____ year(s) in high school.
      (Freshman, sophomore, junior, senior)

125

REQUESTING A LETTER OF RECOMMENDATION

A significant accomplishment I had in your class was:

_____.

(A strongly written paper, oral presentation, mastery of specific topic)
(Be specific and give titles, topics, etc.)

An obstacle I overcame in your class was:

_____.

(Conjugating verbs, factoring, fear of public speaking, etc.)

Something I learned about myself in your class was:

_____.

(How to ask for help, work ethic, leadership, critical thinking, etc.)

Something I want the admission committee to know about me is:

_____.

(My work ethic, personality, ability to multi-task or overcome obstacles, helpfulness,
attitude, capacity to learn new things, etc.)

I am passionate about:

_____.

(Math, robotics, sports, learning, helping others, organizing, choir, etc.)

If there is any other information I can provide you to make this task easier for you, please

let me know. You can contact me at:

_____.

(Email address here)

Thank you again for writing this letter of recommendation. I truly appreciate your time.

_____.

(Your name here)

MY COLLEGE RANKINGS WORKSHEET

In August of your senior year, list your preferred order of colleges you'd like to attend. List them again in December and then in April. This will help you track the order of your list over time.

MY SCHOOL RANKINGS (AUGUST)

1. _____

2. _____

3. _____

4. _____

5. _____

6. _____

MY SCHOOL RANKINGS (DECEMBER)

1. _____

2. _____

3. _____

4. _____

5. _____

6. _____

MY SCHOOL RANKINGS (APRIL)

1. _____

2. _____

3. _____

4. _____

5. _____

6. _____

CHAPTER 10

Step 5:
Paying for College

···················· TIMELINE: ····················
FRESHMAN – SENIOR YEAR (DEPENDING UPON THE TYPE OF AID)

FAFSA (Free Application for Federal Student Aid):
File during October of Student's Senior Year until December of Senior Year
(October is better)

College-sponsored Scholarships:
Apply when applying to individual colleges for admission (deadlines vary)
which usually is Fall of the student's senior year.

Private Scholarships: Freshman Year – End of Senior Year:
Can be started during any time during high school years depending upon
each scholarship's criteria.

While applying might be the most cumbersome task of the college process, paying for college is certainly the most daunting. I once had a father come to his child's college planning meeting and asked me the cost of a well-known private university in our area. When I told him the cost, he gasped and said, "That's like driving a Lexus off a cliff every year for four years!" In some ways, it's not a bad analogy. It's no secret that the cost of education far exceeds the cost of living and rate of inflation in the United States. The good news is: there is hope if you are willing to be flexible in what your expectation of college looks like and if you are willing to make some sacrifices on amenities, housing, and other expenditures.

While several options on how to pay for college will be listed in this chapter, you might seriously consider enlisting the help of a financial aid professional to help you with your college planning questions. As it relates to filing federal paperwork, you might enlist the help of your financial planner, a college or university's financial aid counselor, or a private educational planner who specializes in financial aid and planning if you are so inclined. While your high school counselor can cover the basics, financial aid can be complicated and messy and, at some point, you may need to call in the experts. So many circumstantial factors influence financial aid reporting including divorce, death, situations involving non-custodial parents, job loss, etc. The list goes on and on. Since nearly every person's situation is different, you will want to talk to someone to have those individual questions answered before you complete any paperwork

I think it's fair to say nearly everyone has sticker shock when they look at the price of college. It's not uncommon to see sticker prices of $40,000-$60,000+ per year for private colleges. Before you faint, know that number is what is called the "Cost of Attendance" (COA) and it can be reduced. The COA is the total cost to attend the university including tuition, room, board, fees, and books. Often, however, students will be able to reduce their COA by qualifying for financial aid and/or scholarships. So, before you knock a school off your list because of the sticker price, I would encourage you to use the Net Price Calculator (NPC) feature that is found on colleges' websites. A Net Price Calculator estimates the cost of attendance for a student at a specific university after scholarships and financial aid. This is what is called the "net price." To determine it, you take a school's total cost of attendance and subtract from it amounts awarded for scholarships and/or financial aid. This can vary widely from school to school.

To use the NPC, you as a family will enter all your personal data on the school's NPC forms online. Once this is done, the program gives an *estimate* of what the student's out-of-pocket expenses may be. They will ask questions about grades and scores to estimate scholarship eligibility, and they will ask questions about your financial status to determine if you might qualify for financial aid based on your needs. Every school's NPC is different, so you will have to complete the form on each individual school's website you are interested in attending. This will allow you to take a closer look at your estimated bottom line of what you might be paying for each college. This information will allow you to make an informed decision. Remember the information you enter provides an ESTIMATE of your costs. It does not guarantee the exact amount you will receive, but calculators are pretty accurate. You will still need to apply for the scholarships and complete your federal financial aid forms (as well as any others required by the individual college), but it gives you some good data upfront so you have an idea of what your out-of-pocket expenses might be in the end. To use a school's net price calculator, simply look online at the school's website under financial aid.

When we look at the financial component, there are essentially three ways to pay for college:

1) Your own cold hard-earned cash (savings and 529 savings programs)

2) Scholarships (private and college-based)

3) Financial Aid (including grants, loans, and work-study)

Cash relies on your own discipline and ability to have saved over the years. The second option, scholarships, relies on merit. That is, a student met a certain set of criteria that resulted in the financial award in the form of a scholarship that will not ever need to be repaid. The third option, financial aid, may or may not have to be repaid depending on the type of award made.

CASH

The first is self-explanatory (and often elusive). To pay the bill, you can simply dip into your cash savings (like I said, elusive) or, if you've started a special savings plan for college tuition (called a 529 plan), you will utilize this fund when the time comes for paying college bills. A 529 program works for funding college a lot like a 401k works for funding retirement. The money is earmarked specifically for college and is often invested in the market while a child is young and withdrawn when the child is 18 and enrolls in college. To learn more about 529 savings plans, you can easily find more online, and most states have a 529 program in place. You can invest, however, in any 529 program you would like that seems to be a good fit for you. Your financial planner or a college's financial aid officer can also help you sift through the investment options.

PAYING FOR COLLEGE WITH SCHOLARSHIPS

Scholarships are essentially free money and the best way to fund a college education. They don't need to be repaid, and most colleges will allow you to 'stack' scholarships. What this means is that you can have multiple scholarships from multiple sources (college or privately funded scholarships) and it will lower your out-of-pocket costs. You can usually do this so long as your scholarships do not exceed the total of the school bill. There are two types of scholarships up for grabs: college and private. Let's talk about college scholarships first.

COLLEGE SCHOLARSHIPS

College scholarships are usually partial-tuition scholarships that the school provides the student and are based on merit. That is, the student meets some sort of criteria (usually academic) that, when met, will award him or her a financial stipend. As an example, Johnny applies to a private college with a 3.75 GPA and a 27 on his ACT. Based on these criteria, the private college awards him a $10,000 renewable scholarship. Let's say Johnny also applies to a public state college at the same time. That college, in turn, awards him a $1,000 renewable scholarship. Why the substantial difference? Scholarships at private universities are mostly funded by institutional funds (private money they have in their own pockets) while public universities rely on tax dollars. Because private institutions have more financial freedom with how they spend their money (and sometimes more resources), they can sometimes offer bigger scholarships.

However, keep in mind that public institutions subsidize a student's tuition costs, so the cost for a student to attend a public university is much less than a private school where the entire tuition cost is passed on to the student. Either way, at the end of the day, families must look at the bottom line and see who is giving them the best deal. A large scholarship from a private school can sometimes make a bigger dent in the bottom line even though the initial sticker price is higher. I have seen some students attend a private school cheaper than a public school. For that reason, I encourage families to look at both public and private school options and not rule anything out until they see the bottom line on their expenses.

A good reminder here is not to put all your eggs in one basket. Much like admission where it's important to spread out your options academically, the same is true financially. This is exactly why you don't want to have schools of all the same price point on your list.

As an example, let's say a student applies to all private schools with $60,000 price tags. The family is counting on scholarships and financial aid to make it possible for the student to attend. Then, let's say that the scholarship package gives them $15,000/year, and financial aid nets them $5,000 in grants. None of that $20,000 will need to be repaid. However, that leaves the family on the hook to pay $40,000/year out of their own pocket. In many cases, the financial aid package may offer a student loan to offset some of that $40K, but that money will still have to be repaid (plus interest). Over the span of four years of college, the student is responsible for paying back $160,000 after graduation. That is the equivalent of a house in some parts of the country.

Scholarships awarded by the college themselves are often renewable funds, and that is what makes them so desirable. That means if the student keeps up his or her end of the bargain—maintaining a certain GPA, playing a sport, or is working towards a certain major, then his or her scholarship will be renewed for subsequent years. To apply for a scholarship, a college will have a student do one of two things: either they will take the information they need to make the scholarship decision directly from their admission application OR they will have the student complete a separate application for the scholarship. Be sure you know what the requirements and deadlines are to be considered for a scholarship! This is an unforgiving process.

Every college notifies students if they have been awarded a partial scholarship at different points in the application process. For example, many colleges will notify a student of a specific scholarship and dollar amount at the same time they notify him or her of admission. Some schools will award admission first and then notify students of scholarships a bit later. Your admission rep can you tell you what his or her respective school's procedure is or you can usually find a timeline on the school's website.

If a student is awarded a partial scholarship and then later the admission office decides a student is worthy of competing for a full-ride scholarship, he or she may receive an additional offer to come and participate in a scholarship competition. Scholarship competitions are usually held during the student's second semester of senior year and will offer half, three-quarter, or full tuition. Some even include room and board as part of their award. Special elite criteria will need to be met for a student to be included in the competition. Some of these factors include quantitative factors such as GPA and ACT while other factors might include nomination by your admission rep or qualities such as leadership positions on your activity list.

Regardless of how you have been chosen to participate, a scholarship competition is always worth your time. In addition to the potential payoff financially, it is a wealth of experience in terms of interviewing practice, networking, and information-gathering. Only a small percentage of the high school population is selected to compete for scholarship competitions, so don't be upset if you aren't selected. And if you are selected, treat it like the bonus round. You can't lose what you've already been awarded; you can only add to it. If you are selected, be sure to enlist the help of interview prep classes at your high school or a trusted individual (like your counselor) who can walk you through the ropes of potential interview questions, explain the format and purpose for scholarship interviews as well as what to wear. Remember, preparation and first impressions make a difference in this part of the process.

In addition to the mainstream freshman college scholarships outlined above, students might also want to dig a bit deeper with the colleges they are interested in to see if the colleges offer **departmental scholarships.** These scholarships can be added on in addition to the general freshman scholarships. These are usually provided to students seeking a specific major and meet specific criteria. Often, these scholarships are reserved for students who are considered a minority. Now before you think "this doesn't apply to me," consider the following scenarios:

A young woman wants to be an engineer, and the engineering department is offering a $500 scholarship to a female engineering student. A young man plans on being a nursing student and the nursing department is offering a scholarship to a male nursing major. Oftentimes, minority is not just race, but minority in a given field. Since the majority of engineering majors are male and nursing majors are female, schools may want to increase the numbers of the opposite gender. Another example might include the student who wants to major in music and the school happens to need a tuba player. If a tuba player comes along, there might be a departmental scholarship there for someone who can fill that niche.

Schools sometimes will offer scholarships to fledgling majors that have just been created to attract quality students to their budding programs. It is always worth a conversation with your admission rep to see if there are any departmental scholarships based on your major. Again, be sure to follow directions and complete any necessary paperwork by the deadline to be considered. Departmental scholarships can always be stacked on top of your freshman scholarship. It is important to note, however, that departmental scholarships will be revoked if you don't stay in the major or maintain the other qualifications of the scholarship

PRIVATE SCHOLARSHIPS

While scholarships awarded by colleges are usually the largest lump sum of money a student will receive, students and parents often overlook private scholarships and the economic impact they can provide. Private scholarships are usually small, but their dollar amounts can add up making a dent in reducing freshman year costs. Private scholarships are often non-renewable or what I like to call a "one-shot deal." Private scholarships are funded by organizations or individuals who want to give back to their community. This can be a variety of places including civic organizations and private companies. Organizations who award scholarships typically award anywhere from $500 to $20,000 with most falling in the $1,000-$2,000 range. You may think, "Well, it's just a thousand dollars. It's not worth applying." But because scholarships from private sources can usually be stacked on top of awards already received from the colleges, winning multiple private scholarships can reduce the freshman year bill. While they are not renewable, it all helps.

To find private scholarships, there are several places to look:

1. REPUTABLE ONLINE SCHOLARSHIP SITES. Free online scholarship search sites exist and can easily be found online. I have put a scholarship search website list at the end of this chapter to help you get started with some of the more reliable sites you may want to utilize. A word of caution, though, about private scholarships: be careful about who you give your information to. There are plenty of scams out there, and you need to be careful with what you are doing. There are also links on the bottom of the scholarship search website list to help you know how to spot scams.

2. PARENTS' EMPLOYERS. Often large employers offer scholarships for employees' children. Check with your company's Human Resources department.

3. YOUR HIGH SCHOOL'S SCHOLARSHIP LISTING. Ask your counselor where this information is posted. These lists also highlight local scholarships offered by the community. This can be an excellent resource for students.

4. STUDENTS CAN ALSO USE APPS ON THEIR PHONES AS A SEARCH MEANS. If you do that, however, you need to consider you will often have to pay for apps. My belief is that you shouldn't have to spend money to get money. I've done a little research on apps and found that what I can access online is just as effective (if not more so) than a phone app. However, if you come across a phone app that works for you then go for it.

As for when to start searching for private scholarships, families can begin as early as the student's freshman year. Most families will find that students are required to be seniors to apply for the bulk of the scholarships available, but there are a few that offer awards to younger students. As far as when the mainstream search should happen, the student should start looking for private scholarships beginning in their junior year of high school and continue to do so until they graduate.

SOME TIPS ON PRIVATE SCHOLARSHIPS

People always ask me what I suggest doing to increase their odds of winning private scholarships. Here are some suggestions:

1. ALWAYS APPLY FOR THE LOCAL SCHOLARSHIP. Local scholarships often have smaller dollar amounts, but they also have smaller pools of applicants. I have seen local scholarships that have as few as eight applicants, which greatly increases the chances of winning. In comparison, large national scholarships may offer up to $20,000, but there are many more applicants (sometimes up to a million) which greatly decrease the odds of winning. I would rather win $500 in a local scholarship than $0 in a national competition.

2. ALWAYS ENTER THE SCHOLARSHIP COMPETITION THAT REQUIRES THE ESSAY. I have seen so many students over the years not enter a scholarship competition because they don't want to write an essay. Because of this, the number of entries is often lower. Scholarship essays don't always have word minimums, so long as what you need to say is succinct and strong, you have as decent a chance as anyone of winning.

I once had a student who wrote a clever 4-word response to an essay prompt and won $2,000.

3. GET YOURSELF ORGANIZED. Get yourself a binder, notebook, folder, or other office supply item that will help you keep track of your deadlines, passwords, and other relevant information. (Use the password log from Chapter 9.)

4. SET A DEDICATED TIME EVERY WEEK TO RESEARCH SCHOLARSHIP LISTINGS. Scholarship applications can sometimes require tedious amounts of detail and short deadlines. To avoid missing anything I first suggest you set a specific time and day each week to look at scholarship listings. (Ex: Every Sunday night before you go to bed.) This keeps you in the loop of what is currently available as soon as it posts. Some scholarships have short turnaround times, so you want to give yourself every advantage in having enough time to complete and submit the application. And, because transcripts or letters of recommendation can also be required, you will need to give yourself enough time to enlist the help of those who will be providing those documents for you.

5. TELL YOUR COUNSELOR YOU ARE LOOKING FOR SCHOLARSHIPS. It may not produce a solid lead, but it never hurts to mention to him or her that you are looking for additional funds for school. Hopefully, when one pops up you will be the first person that comes to mind!

Regardless of where you look for scholarships, it is always crucial that you protect your information. If you use a search engine or website to find potential private scholarships, always remember that safeguarding your critical information such as your social security number is essential. No scholarship committee has any reason to have your social security number. **If you find that a site is asking for personal information such as a social security number, take it as a red flag and move on as a precautionary measure.**

FINANCIAL AID

Most people would rank filing for financial aid right up there with a root canal or the stomach flu. It is not a fun process, and for most people, it's not something they look forward to doing. With that said, it is so necessary to do so (and promptly) because it can make the difference between going to college and not going. My area of expertise is limited here. All the financial aid officers of the world have my respect, as this process can be intimidating. As I mentioned earlier in the book, enlisting the help of a college's financial aid office or your private financial aid expert or financial planner is the best suggestion I can give. This section does offer, however, a basic understanding of financial aid and how the process works.

Financial aid is based on nothing else other than NEED. This is the fact that there is a gap between the cost of the student's education and the family's ability to pay. It has nothing to do with smarts or academic major or athletic talent. Need is established once a gap exists between the bill and the family's resources. So how is need identified? Families will complete what is called a FAFSA (Free Application for Federal Student Aid).

To do this, they will first go to the FAFSA website and create an account and get a PIN (personal identification number). The FAFSA is a free form that every family reading this book should complete. Those wanting to file for federal financial aid should do so in October of the student's senior year. Punctuality is key here. The earliest a senior's family can apply for financial aid is October 1 of the student's senior year. Waiting to file, though, can be costly. Federal financial aid is like a big pot of money, and everyone wants to put their hand in the pot. However, to do this, families must have filed their FAFSA, so don't miss out! Families who wait several months to file may find they qualify for aid, but there is no money left in the pot for them to access if they are late to the game. Many students come up on the short end because of filing their FAFSA late and it has come at quite a price since having no federal aid makes their opportunity vanish. When the money's gone, it's gone, and nothing can change that. The FAFSA form can be found at www.fafsa.ed.gov. (Note: Families should use only the official FAFSA website listed above and no other. Other sites may have the information, but ask you to pay to complete the form or may be a scam site collecting your personal information.)

The FAFSA requires the completion of information including family demographics, social security numbers, income, assets, and liabilities using what is called prior-prior year tax information. An easy way to understand this is to back up two years from the student's graduation year to determine what tax returns to use. As an example, a student who will graduate in 2022 will use 2020 tax returns to file their first year FAFSA. Once you complete the FAFSA form, the government will do their number crunching, and the family's Expected Family Contribution (EFC) is established. EFC's can range from zero (full need) to 99,999 (no need). The EFC is the dollar amount that the government formula has determined a family can afford to put towards a child's education annually. **Let's look at an example:**

Susie is currently beginning her senior year in high school. Her parents know that October is prime time to complete the FAFSA. So, they go online and answer all the questions (including reporting what colleges Susie has applied to so they can receive her FAFSA information to award her financial aid package to her). Once the family has completed their FAFSA, they will receive notification of what their EFC is for the upcoming year. Let's say that their EFC is $20,000. That means that the expectation is there that Susie's family will be able to fund her education (for the first year) to the tune of $20,000 out of their own pocket. If school is $40,000 and Susie receives a scholarship for $15,000 (merit based—not need), then she is still on the hook for $25,000. The expectation is that they will pay the $20,000 themselves and the college will work to find the remaining $5,000 for her. Now, the school may award her a grant (which does not need to be repaid), but more than likely they will offer her a loan of $5,000. While the loan is great in the short term, it is imperative that families remember that loans always need to be repaid. Student loan debt is a growing concern in the United States with some students owing as much as $300,000! That is an insurmountable number and totally will void the value of having an education at that point.

Many schools (high schools and colleges) have FAFSA completion workshops which have you bring your tax forms and other paperwork, and they will walk you through how to set up a FAFSA account and answer any questions you may have. These workshops are extremely helpful, and they are free.

Many colleges also offer online chat times where you can ask questions about your FAFSA completion in the event you can't make it to campus. One other note, colleges who offer FAFSA completion workshops or chats don't require a student be applying to their university to be able to participate. It is simply a free service offered as community outreach. Take advantage of what is offered locally in your community! Parents, if you are interested in attending a financial aid workshop, simply inquire with your child's high school or your area college to see when one might be offered.

Often, there are special circumstances that arise where the information gathered as part of the FAFSA process does not accurately reflect the family's current financial picture. Because the data used for your family's FAFSA is nearly two years old, a lot can change. If you've had special circumstances such as a job loss, catastrophic illness, or medical expenses, it may be worth completing a special circumstances form at each college you are applying. By doing this, you may explain your current financial circumstances directly to the colleges. They will then consider your situation and use professional judgment to decide if they can offer additional aid. Be sure to do this, however, early in the senior year as soon as you know your FAFSA EFC. Schools have limited funds. Contact your prospective colleges' financial aid offices EARLY in the college application process, so you don't miss out. Remember that some situations are not worthy of special circumstances including buying yourself a boat, sending your child to a private high school, or getting a vacation home. This is for extenuating circumstances, not personal choices.

When you are looking for dollars for college, look under every rock and pursue every avenue that gives you funds that do not have to be repaid before taking loans. In the event you decide to take a loan, you need to look at the big picture of living expenses after graduation. Students (and sometimes parents) often look at a loan and think "It's only $12,000. It can be repaid once I start working after graduation." Maybe, but when you multiply the $12,000 by four years, you are looking at nearly $50,000 in debt that must be repaid. Unlike bankruptcy or home foreclosures, educational debt follows you to the grave. You cannot escape it once you have signed the dotted line. And, if you happen to be a parent who thinks you'll co-sign for a loan and Junior will be responsible for repayment, think again.

If Junior decides to stop repaying his loans, doesn't find a job, or runs away to Hawaii to be a professional surfer, then you are on the hook to pay the loan back yourself. Every. Stinking. Dime. If you are a parent who wants to do right by your child, be sure to take care of yourself and your retirement fund as much as you can. Saving for retirement makes sure that not only are you covered in your later years, but your child will not be responsible for your care or fiscal needs. If push comes to shove, it would be better they have some student loan debt than you bankrupt yourself with loans at the expense of your financial stability in old age. Students have more time to work and more time to live than parents usually do. Be smart about it, though, no matter who's paying. Just food for thought.

In addition to the total dollar amount borrowed, you also need to consider other factors such as whether the student will want to continue his or her education and get a graduate degree (more costs), how much money will they earn in his or her given major, as well as cost of living expenses. Let's break this down to explain each of these considerations.

First, if a student knows from the beginning of the college search process that an advanced degree (graduate school, law school, medical school, etc.) is even a remote possibility, they need to pay attention to the debt they are racking up (or cash funds they are spending) at the undergraduate level. I have seen many a wise student choose the less expensive route for undergrad so they could have funds available for graduate school. I've also seen people break the bank at the undergraduate level to have the 'name brand' school only to be broke when it comes time for graduate school. They forge ahead, postponing repayment of previous school loans because they will still be in school, only to have to face the music later as the debt load continues to mount.

In the second scenario, you must consider the student's major and income potential for a given degree. It's no secret that social workers, for example, are some of the most poorly paid majors on the planet while engineers, pharmacists, and physical therapists may have an easier time finding a well-paying job. People who have majors with less capacity for large paychecks or job opportunities need to be even more aware of any debt they are incurring. That's not to say engineers or health care workers should get crazy with their debt, but common sense needs to prevail. There is always the possibility that any student can graduate in a recession with little hope of landing a job and yet still will need to begin repaying debt six months after graduation—job or no job.

Another factor people need to consider when taking on debt is what I like to call "the big picture." A student might look at $50,000 worth of debt and think "It's only 50K and I have ten years to pay it off. I'll have a job, so I can knock that out no problem." What they are not considering is the other monetary factors that will influence how your paycheck gets spent. Things like food, a mortgage, transportation, insurance, utilities. The list goes on forever. You don't know what part of the country you'll get your first job, and you may need every red cent just to pay the rent if you're in an area with a high cost of living—much less being able to buy a house before you're 40. Life is expensive. Period.

MAKING COLLEGE LESS EXPENSIVE

So how do you avoid massive debt load? I have a few suggestions you may or may not like, but if you truly want to look at long-term financial security, it starts by tightening the belt now.

1. CONSIDER A COMMUNITY COLLEGE FOR THE FIRST TWO YEARS OF COLLEGE. This will give the student a much cheaper option for the first two years. The student can live at home (saving room and board costs). The price tag even without a scholarship is much more doable. The key is knowing where you want to transfer to after graduation from the community college and get yourself a good adviser at the community college who can help you with picking the right courses. I always hear people say that "certain community college courses" don't transfer to the four-year school. There are two things here I think are important to understand:

One, remedial courses (those below the 100 level freshman courses—think Beginning Algebra versus College Algebra) never count toward a degree at any college. You must meet the minimum rigor level of a given subject. Be sure to understand that if you need remedial courses, they won't count towards your degree regardless of where you take them. Secondly, I find when you transfer your entire two-year degree to a four-year college you have much more success of credits being accepted at a four-year college. It's sort of like a package deal. Get an associate degree in general studies (or general transfer studies), and you'll have covered most, if not all, of your general education requirements. This will leave your last two years at your four-year institution for classes in your major. And, you get the same diploma as someone else at graduation so no employer would ever know you spent the first two years at community college and saved yourself a lot of money.

2. DUAL ENROLL IN COLLEGE COURSES OR TAKE ADVANCED PLACEMENT COURSES IN HIGH SCHOOL. Students who enroll in Advanced Placement (AP) courses and score high enough on their standardized AP tests can get advanced credit in college as can those students who take courses through their high schools for college credit. This puts students in a favorable position to have some (if not all) of their credits transfer to their college. Doing this reduces the number of courses a student needs to take in college which may allow them to graduate a semester or two early which saves a ton of cash. It's probably worth noting here that AP courses (with the proper score) are more universally accepted than dual enrollment courses from a local college. Make sure you ask your potential colleges what they will accept. The tough part here is that students must make decisions about dual enrollment and AP courses for the junior and senior year long before the student knows where they will attend college. This makes for a challenging dilemma on what road to take. Do as much research as possible early on, and you will have more chance of your credit transferring to the school of your choice.

3. LOOK FOR A SCHOOL THAT WILL AFFORD YOU MORE SCHOLARSHIP MONEY. The trick to this is to make yourself look like Einstein. If you have a 24 on your ACT, look for schools whose average may be 21 or 22. If you have a 30, look at institutions with averages of 26 or 27. You always want to look smarter than the average bear. Strategically selecting a school where you are the 'smart' kid will probably get you more scholarship money, because they want to attract the students that will up their average score on campus. What you do not want to do is select a school for the full ride that will in no way challenge you. If you have a 33 and go to a school whose average is 21, you will be bored out of your mind, and you will waste your education because you won't be challenged enough. You want to be a little smarter, but not so much so that you could teach the class.

4. CONSIDER A PUBLIC INSTITUTION WITH AN HONORS COLLEGE. State schools have some of the least expensive (in-state) tuition rates. Parents will often complain to me that they are afraid it is too big, not challenging enough or that their student will get lost in the crowd. If that is the case, look for a public school who has an honors college. An honors college works much like the honors track in high school. You get to take specific courses other mainstream students don't get to take that offer more rigor, more in-depth curriculum and discussion, and have smaller class enrollments. Honors students may also have preferred housing options that house them with other honor students or in quiet dorms. An Honors College will likely have higher criteria to get into their programs, so check to see what ACT or SAT requirements, GPA or other admission requirements must be met for admission. The Honors College is often a second step in the admission process. Students will be admitted to the university at large first then must file a second application to be selected to the honors college.

143

Honors college programs do not usually cost the student any additional money but give a lot of bang for the buck.

5. LOOK FOR SCHOOLS THAT OFFER TUITION LOCKS. In answer to the rising cost of tuition, some schools now offer tuition locks. What that means is that if you start a college your freshman year with tuition that costs $40,000 per year, you will never see a tuition increase for each of your remaining years. This is a huge saving when you consider you could see tuition hikes averaging 3-7% annually if you couldn't lock in a set tuition rate.

6. COMMUTE. I know this makes a lot of students cringe because they fear they'll be 'missing out' on college life, but commuting to campus in your hometown each day will easily save $8,000-$10,000 per academic year. You may not think you want this option, but it is quite the money saver.

7. CONSIDER THE MILITARY TO HELP FUND YOUR EDUCATION. Military programs such as ROTC, which require enlisting after graduation, can sometimes help finance your education. Yes, there is a service commitment on your part that might entail dedicating years of your life to the military, but some people find this a viable option to funding their education and starting their careers. It's not for everyone, but it is for some. If you are interested in ROTC, contact your college of choice to see if this is an option on their campus.

Like I said at the beginning of this chapter, financial aid can be daunting. But by utilizing your resources and enlisting the help of others as well as asking good questions and getting creative about your options to pay for college, your due diligence can go a long way in making the dream of having an affordable education a reality.

ACTION STEPS
for Chapter 10

PAYING FOR COLLEGE

1) Use the net price calculator on each school's website you are considering attending to determine what your costs might be.

2) Apply for each college's freshman scholarships by the deadline (usually fall of senior year).

3) Use reputable search engines to seek and apply for private scholarships.

4) Set a specific weekly schedule of when you will actively look for private scholarships.

5) Apply for federal aid (FAFSA) during fall of senior year.

6) Explore options to make college less expensive.

WORKSHEETS FOR CHAPTER 10

COLLEGE SCHOLARSHIP SEARCH SITES

Big Future   www.bigfuture.collegeboard.org/scholarship-search

Cappex   www.cappex.com

College Net   www.collegenet.com

College Niche   colleges.niche.com/scholarships/

*Fastweb   www.fastweb.com

FinAid   www.finaid.org

My Scholly   www.myscholly.com

Sallie Mae   www.salliemae.org

Scholarships.com   www.scholarships.com

Scholarship Expert   www.scholarshipexperts.com

Super College   www.supercollege.com

Chegg.com   www.chegg.com/scholarships

> **⋯ TIP ⋯**
>
> *If you question a scholarship's credibility and are wanting to check to see if it is a scam, check with the Better Business Bureau (www.bbb.com).*
>
> *You can also go to the Department of Education's website at www.studentaid.ed.gov/ students/publications/lsa/index.html to learn more about spotting scholarship scams.*

NOTE: CCT does not endorse or recommend any one scholarship website. Individuals should always exercise caution when using websites that ask for personal information.

CHAPTER 11

Step 6: Deciding Which College to Attend

Of all the information I share about the college process, the timeline for making a decision about college is often the most surprising to students and parents. Families often assume that their student will need to make a knee-jerk, fast-acting decision once the acceptance letters come. While there are a few exceptions to this rule, students must notify the schools they will be attending (as well as the schools they are declining) by May 1 of the student's graduating year. This is what is known in the industry as the **National Reply Date.** By this date, everyone needs to make their final decision. **By May 1 of your senior year, you must notify (preferably in writing) the school you will be attending of your decision to enroll. You will need to notify every school you've chosen NOT to attend your decision as well.**

If you don't convey to a school by May 1 you are accepting its offer of admission and financial aid package, it is free to give your seat, your bed, and any financial aid or scholarship money you may have had to another incoming student. **Don't forget, though, that (in most cases) you need to secure housing far in advance of the May 1 deadline.** This often means making a security deposit (most are refundable) once an offer of admission has been made. See the reminder in the Action Step box in Chapter 9. On the flip side, notifying the colleges you will NOT be coming is important too. Often, schools have waiting lists of students who want to attend but haven't yet been admitted as well as housing and financial aid awards to consider. When you let a college know you won't be coming, you may be helping another student realize their dream of attending college. It is a lot of logistics on the part of the college to figure out who's enrolling, so you are helping them as well.

Some colleges accept nearly three to four times the students for which they have the room. They realize that about one-quarter to one-third of the accepted applicants will take them up on their offer while the others will choose another option. Colleges will over-accept because they need to fill their bed and desk space. If they have room for 1,000 freshmen and only offer admission to 1,000, they will end up on the short end of the stick. Now, there will be some exceptions to this rule at more elite colleges who probably don't get turned down often, but more than likely your school will over-accept for its incoming freshman class.

What's the big deal, then, if I don't reply in time, you ask? Well, if students do not notify the school of their intent to enroll, they may find themselves last in line for classes or without a bed to sleep in. I recall a school that several years ago didn't hear from many students about their intention to enroll after being accepted. The school moved on to accepting other students to fill the seats, and when the students showed up in August, those who had not communicated they were coming were flat out refused because they literally had nowhere for them to go. It was a hard lesson for those students. Don't let the same happen to you. Be sure that you notify schools in writing of your decision, so you have a paper trail as well as a seat in the class and a bed to sleep in when you get there.

What happens then when a school offers acceptance to students and more accept than the number of bed or desk spaces they have available? Well, that's happened too. I distinctly remember on more than one occasion where a school had to open old dorms or triple up students in a room. One school put its overflow of students up at the Holiday Inn until they could fast-forward on a dorm under construction and have it ready to go by the second semester. If that happens, though, and you've conveyed your intention to attend, then that becomes the school's problem to make good on course offerings and find bed space for the overflow.

I mentioned there were exceptions to the May 1 response deadline. The biggest of these are **early decision applicants.** Remember that early decision applicants are under a binding contract. Because they will find out earlier than most applicants of their acceptances and because they have a contractual obligation to enroll if accepted, an early decision applicant will be locked in well in advance of the May 1 deadline.

IF YOU CAN'T DECIDE WHERE TO GO

Let's talk a little bit about the indecisive student who knows that May 1 is looming and doesn't know which of their schools to attend. This is a common dilemma among high school seniors. For some, it is splitting hairs between two schools, and they are sometimes paralyzed by the fear of making a 'wrong' decision. Usually, by March of senior year, students have all the information they need to make a solid decision. They know where they have been accepted, they know their scholarship and financial aid awards and are prepared for the costs involved, and they've most likely visited the various campuses. Yet, after all this information has been gathered, they often come up stuck. This is usually when students show up at my office door, stressed about the first major life decision before them, worried they are going to mess it all up.

If there is one point I would like to make clear here, it is that students need to remember they can be happy in more than one place. This is true for most of life's decisions. You can love more than one house you buy, be successful in more than one job, or be equally happy with either car you choose to purchase. There is no utopia in life. It is often a series of choices and roads not taken. Sometimes, those who struggle with where to go for college make better decisions than those who enter their post-secondary experience with blinders on throughout the process. They do not want to consider other scenarios or options when the time to explore is open to them. The thought of having another option overwhelms them, so they go with what they know and seek that one college with tunnel vision. They may appear to have it all together at the moment (which often frustrates the undecided), but I have seen many of those students who never wavered (or explored) in their college decision process transfer after just a semester or two because the image they built up in their mind didn't quite materialize. There is a silver lining for those who struggle. They often do more research and look for red flags. They often understand by the end of the process that they make as informed a decision as possible and then take the leap of faith it will work out.

So, what do you do when you are stuck between two colleges and time is marching towards the National Reply Date? Here are some suggestions:

1. MAKE A LIST OF PROS AND CONS FOR EACH SCHOOL. Sometimes just getting thoughts out of your head and onto a piece of paper can be extremely helpful in lowering stress. Being able to take a concrete look at what the good, bad, and the ugly are for each school can help you see things more clearly.

2. REVISIT THE COLLEGES IN QUESTION. Students taking a second (or even third) look at a college will often see things with different eyes. Since a considerable amount of time has probably passed since their last visit and they are focused in on specific qualities they want in a college, they will often zero in on attributes they want or get an intuitive feeling they belong at one school more than the other. Even something as simple as a rainy day can tip the scales. You may see things more clearly the second time around.

3. TALK TO OTHERS WHO ALREADY GO THERE (OR WHO HAVE TRANSFERRED). This is a risky move. While it is one way to gather information, you must remember it is subjective information. One person's experience of loving—or hating—an institution may not be the same for you. Take the information you have regarding another person's experience with a grain of salt or at least look for other students having similar experiences to validate what one person's opinion is.

4. LIVE AS IF... This approach has worked for many students I have worked with over the years. While the mind tends to bounce back and forth between "I'll go to School X" to "Maybe School Y" in a matter of thoughts, I encourage students to 'live as if....' In this approach, I ask students to live for 24 hours as if they have decided to go to School X. Act as if the decision has been made. Live it. Don't think about it. Don't dwell on or question it. But, do pay attention to how you feel about this decision. Do you have a sense of peace or good feeling about it? Or do you feel anxious or have red flags coming to mind? Once you've lived with School X as your decision for 24 hours, switch your decision to School Y for 24 hours and then repeat the process above. At the end of the process, compare notes. You'll often see your intuition nudging you in one direction or the other.

5. IF MONEY IS AN ISSUE, TALK TO THE FINANCIAL AID OFFICE. If you find you are short on cash to attend a specific school, have a civil conversation with them. Schools will usually lay their best offer on the table from the beginning. However, let's say a family runs their numbers and knows they need another $3,000 to make this happen. They should let the school know. What you don't want to do is handle the situation like buying a car; giving ultimatums, comparing offers, and threatening to walk away. I can pretty well assure you they will bid you farewell without a second glance. I know this because I have seen it happen.

There are usually a couple of scenarios in which colleges respond well. One, if they know their school is the student's number one choice. Secondly, if you can give them an EXACT dollar amount you need to make the first year happen. That doesn't mean you'll get another dime. It just means they know you really want to be there, and they know you've done your homework. In this situation, they will probably be more than willing to have a conversation with you and take a second look. Sincerity and honesty go a long way in this process. If you're having a difficult time making a decision because you have your heart set on your number one school and the money isn't there, have a conversation with financial aid before you walk away. Based on that conversation and the outcome, you'll know if this door is open or closed.

6. TALK TO A COUNSELOR. This isn't heavy-duty therapy we are talking about, but if you find yourself at a stuck point, enlist the help of a counselor. It can be your high school counselor, with whom you've had a working relationship for the last several months or years, or you can solicit the help of a trained counselor outside of school who can listen and give feedback as well as ask some objective questions to help you find your true north.

Remember that, regardless of which tactics you use from the list above, seeking help early is imperative. If you find yourself stuck, you might start this process early in the second semester of the student's senior year. Whatever you do, don't wait until April 30 to seek help to make a May 1 decision. It will only create more stress. Plus, it leaves the potential for a poor decision by waiting until the last minute. Remember some feeling of fear and anxiety is normal with change. Having a moment of trepidation doesn't mean the decision is wrong. It's normal to feel a bit of angst and butterflies. It takes a while to settle into the commitment you're about to make. But, if you're feeling unsettled in a not-so-good way, it may be time to enlist the help of an objective third party who can help you rifle through your feelings about the decision at hand.

Lastly, remember that no choice is permanent. If you've done your research up to this point, you will probably make a good choice, but you can always change your mind. It's important to remind you again that you can be happy in more than one place so it doesn't have to be an 'all or none' decision. Relax and go with your gut. Intuition is a wonderful gift. And once you've decided, enjoy the glory. Spring is a magical time and one of celebration of all the hard work that has been accomplished in four years' time. Relish. Every. Minute.

ACTION STEPS
for Chapter 11

DECIDING WHICH COLLEGE TO ATTEND

IF YOU ARE UNDECIDED:

1) Make a list of pros/cons for each school in consideration.

2) Revisit colleges in question.

3) Gather more information from others to make an informed decision.

4) Make an appointment to talk things over with a counselor.

5) Fully understand the financial obligations at each school to have an exact dollar amount of costs you will be responsible for paying.

FOR EVERYONE….

6) Inform each college you will / will not be attending by May 1 deadline.

7) Don't forget housing contracts, tuition deposits, course registrations, and all the other 'to-do's' the college will remind you to do to be an enrolled student.

8) Arrange to have your final high school transcript (also showing you graduated) as well as any transcripts from colleges at which you were dually enrolled along with AP scores to the college you will be attending.

Section 3:
Additional Information

CHAPTER 12

Special Circumstances: Gap Years, Athletes, Performers, Art Majors, and Learning Differences

I've saved this chapter for all the snippets of information for those who have specific scenarios that may not apply to everyone reading this book. These scenarios include what to do if you are wanting to take a year off between high school and college (called a gap year), if you are an athlete wanting to play college sports, a performer interested in auditions or a potential art major or if you have learning differences that may require you look for special programs or support services. If none of these situations apply to you, you can skip this chapter entirely and move on to the closing thoughts.

GAP YEAR

Gap years are a relatively new concept in the world of post-secondary education but are gaining momentum in popularity. Who wouldn't love to take a year off after all the hard work of high school, sleep in, and travel the world? If that's your idea of a gap year, though, you are probably mistaken. While you can do those things, it won't prepare you for the next step in your education. Gap years are designed to be productive, educational experiences that can be useful in widening your horizons, knowing yourself and talents, and giving back to the community. Probably the most famous of gap years in recent memory is that of Malia Obama, who decided to take a year off after high school to do an internship before enrolling at Harvard.

GUIDELINE TO CREATING A GAP YEAR EXPERIENCE

Gap years can be designed in a variety of ways, and there is no right or wrong. There is, however, good and not-so-good. A gap year should have a focus that will make the student more marketable, mature, and experienced when they do enter college. If an admission professional were to ask you what you did, learned, or produced during your gap year and you spent your year sleeping in, catching up on Netflix, and working your part-time job, it may be a hard sell. Your time needs to be educational, cultural, or civic-minded. You can make a gap year designed solely around volunteering projects or career exploration. You might use the time to become fluent in a new language or enroll in a formal gap year program sponsored by a college or university. The possibilities are endless. Here are some guidelines to consider when designing a gap year:

1) **ASK YOURSELF WHAT YOU WANT THE GAP YEAR TO ACCOMPLISH** (service, education, career exploration, learning a new language, travel, etc.). Your gap year should be personally designed by you but should be structured and have a definite, formal plan.

2) **STRONGLY CONSIDER APPLYING TO COLLEGE DURING YOUR SENIOR YEAR SO YOU HAVE AN ADMISSION SOMEWHERE THAT YOU CAN DEFER.** This way you have an 'in' at a college when you return. The college application process is geared to high school seniors so you will get more support now than when you've graduated high school and are doing it on your own later. Also, applying to college when you are supposed to will leave that door open in the event you decide a gap year isn't for you.

3) **CONSIDER TAKING INTEREST INVENTORIES, DOING INFORMATIONAL INTERVIEWS, OR GOING TO COUNSELING** if you are unsure of what career path you might want if that is part of what you want the gap year to accomplish.

4) **CONSIDER USING YOUR GAP YEAR TO EDUCATE YOURSELF** about educational options including majors, trade school apprenticeships, etc.

5) **DECIDE HOW MUCH YOU ARE WILLING TO PAY FINANCIALLY** for formal programs if you decide to go that route.

6) **CONSIDER A BLEND OF OPTIONS FOR YOUR HOME CITY**—4 months of volunteer work; 4 months of employment; 4 months of auditing classes at a local college, etc. OR consider working full-time for the first six months to fund the formal travel program the last six months.

7) **HAVE AN IDEA OF WHAT YOU MIGHT LIKE TO DO AFTER YOUR GAP YEAR** and ask yourself how your gap year will be helpful. (How would it look to an employer? Will it

help me decide what I want to be? How would it look in the college admissions process?)

QUESTIONS TO ASK WHEN LOOKING AT GAP YEAR OPTIONS

Not all gap year programs are created equal, so you will want to ask these important questions (along with any others you would like to ask) when you are investigating various programs that may be a fit for you. This is especially important given the proximity to home may be a considerable distance, and you want to be sure safety is addressed along with additional costs and fees. Here are a few questions you might want to ask if the student is traveling out of the area and especially out of the country:

1) If the student travels abroad (or out of the area), ask about safety issues, supervision, liability, contacting information, emergencies, etc.

2) Ask for detail information on the fine print—costs, obligations, etc.

3) Ask about stipends, scholarships, financial obligations, etc. to cover the costs

4) Ask about healthcare coverage, immunizations/shots, and travel documents needed

PLACES TO LOOK IF YOU WANT TO CREATE A VOLUNTEER GAP EXPERIENCE

If you want to make volunteer service a portion (or all) of your gap year experience, you will find there are many options out there for either full-time immersion experiences or daily and weekly opportunities locally. You probably already are familiar with some opportunities in your local community, but here are a few you may want to investigate to help get you started:

AmeriCorps / City Year (will usually pay students a stipend + provide housing): www.nationalservice.gov/programs/americorps

Catholic Volunteer Network: catholicvolunteernetwork.org

Volunteer Match: www.volunteermatch.org

Volunteer Odyssey: www.volunteerodyssey.com (Memphis-based)

HandsOn Network: www.pointsoflight.org/handsonnetwork

Idealist.org: www.idealist.org

WHERE TO GET MORE INFORMATION ON FORMAL GAP YEAR PROGRAMS

If you'd like to learn more about gap years, there are a few suggestions you may want to investigate. There is a handbook available called the Guide to Gap Year Programs (eguides.teenlife.com/gap/) you may want to check out. This site also has blogs to read and a database of formal programs to research. Additionally, the book *Gap to Great* by Andrea Wien outlines the advantages of taking a gap year before you enroll in college. You might also want to check out the American Gap Association's website at www.americangap.org to learn more. Educating yourself about all your options is the best way to make an informed and smart decision.

FINANCIAL AID FOR GAP YEAR PROGRAMS

To find financial aid for programs that cost to attend go to the American Gap website at americangap.org/financial-aid.php.

If you are unsure of what your gap year design might look like, enlist the opinions of college admission representatives or other college professionals to see what a successful design might look like. Be warned, though, that a gap year is not for everyone. It requires a significant amount of self-discipline, maturity, and follow-through. For some students who take time off from formal education, the tendency to not go back to school is high. Be certain you have a detailed, exact plan that has a purpose and you have a defined goal for college enrollment after your gap year has ended. You don't want your gap year to turn into a 'gap' in your education long-term.

ATHLETICS

If you are a high school athlete wanting to play sports at the college level, the one thing you must do is keep your grades up consistently. You must fulfill the academic rules and requirements to be able to play sports at the college level. If you do not meet those academic benchmarks, you will not be eligible to play. It will also be a red flag to coaches. Even if they know you have the athletic talent to play and want you as part of their program, you are a big risk if they can't count on you to be academically qualified. Academic requirements aren't just there to get you in the door, you must continue to make grades and accrue college credits to stay eligible to compete.

If you are an athlete who does not have the grades, find tutors, teachers, and good friends who can help you stay focused and on track. It's no different than having a pitching coach, trainer, or other athletic professional to help you reach your athletic goals. Having the support of others will keep you accountable and on track. If you are early in your high school career, make the connections now. Many an athlete has told me that once they made the connection that success in the classroom requires the same routine, discipline, and work ethic as succeeding in sports, their academic success took off as well.

PLAYING NCAA DIVISION I AND II SPORTS

If you want to play a sport and receive an athletic scholarship in the National Collegiate Athletic Association (NCAA) at either Division I or II, you must register with and be certified as an eligible player through the NCAA Eligibility Center. There are academic requirements that must be met in terms of the level of courses taken, the number of credits received, and grades. If you are a student-athlete who is interested in even the possibility of college-level sports, start freshman year to keep your grades up and find out what courses you need to take to keep you eligible. Have a conversation with your high school counselor and/or athletic director as well as go to the Eligibility Center's website (www.eligibilitycenter.org) to learn what the requirements are to play sports at the college level.

You can open an account and register with the NCAA Eligibility Center as early as your sophomore year, but because you need a 6th-semester transcript, you cannot send your grades for evaluation until the end of your junior year. In many cases, students will do both their registration with the Eligibility Center and send their transcript at the end of the junior year unless their recruitment process dictates otherwise. Once you are registered and have your grades on file, coaches will then be able to see if you are academically eligible to play at a given level based on your academic record. They may then be interested in pursuing you as a recruit. While most coaches will be looking for talent earlier than the end of junior year, the grades on file must include the first six semesters of work and so you cannot complete your file any earlier than before six semesters of grades are sent.

A portion of a student's eligibility is based on ACT or SAT scores. Therefore, students must also submit their ACT or SAT scores to the NCAA Eligibility Center. Students will need to formally send their scores. You do this by going back to your ACT or SAT account online and requesting your scores be sent to the NCAA Eligibility Center (Their code is 9999). You do this just like you would when sending your scores to colleges as part of the application process for admission.

The last piece of this puzzle is sending your FINAL transcript when you graduate from high school. This final transcript will allow the Eligibility Center to see you have completed the last requirements of your courses. As an example, they will see you've completed your fourth year of English required and any other required courses you had yet to complete. They also need to see that you graduated! Arrange with your high school counselor to have your transcripts sent as soon as possible after graduation so your file is complete and you can remain eligible to play the following year.

Rules can change from time to time, so the best way to stay up-to-date on any changes in rules and regulations regarding NCAA athletic eligibility is to go directly to the NCAA Eligibility Center's website at www.eligibilitycenter.org. There you will find instructions, flowcharts, and other tips for making yourself eligible to play competitive college sports at the NCAA Division I and II levels.

PLAYING NAIA SPORTS

If you are interested in playing sports for the National Association of Intercollegiate Athletics (NAIA) in college, a similar process to the NCAA is also in place. If you go to their website, you can learn more about registering, requirements to be eligible, and even find showcase events where you can demonstrate your talent as an athlete for recruiters and coaches. (To send your ACT or SAT scores to NAIA, use code 9876.) Go to www.playnaia.org to learn more. Again, rules change, so you always want to go directly to the website to get the most accurate information.

FINAL THOUGHTS ON PLAYING SPORTS IN COLLEGE

Playing athletics competitively at the college level always adds a new wrinkle to the college admission process. In addition to being admitted to the college academically, the college must also want you athletically. It becomes a more intricate process to check off both boxes, and it can take some time for a student-athlete to find what they want academically AND athletically AND the college to want them both academically and athletically. For this reason, I often have my students make two wish lists—one that involves athletics as part of the equation and one that does not. This frustrates many students because they interpret it as a 'you don't think I can do this.' My faith in your athleticism has nothing to do with it. In reality, we all need a backup plan. You never know when you're going to blow out your knee, have a career-ending concussion, or burn out on the sport entirely. Regardless of where your athletic career may (or may not) take you, you will also need an educational plan that will take you to the next step in your life, and your education should always be your primary focus. Your brain will hold out a lot longer in life than your ability to be a competitive athlete.

If you are serious about playing college-level sports or if you just want to pursue gathering more information to see if you want to play college-level sports, I strongly encourage you to ask others for their help and expertise. These people should be able to guide you through this process and give you direction and information. These resources include your high school athletic director, your high school coach, select team coach, and your school counselor. I also strongly recommend you attend informational events regarding athletic eligibility for NCAA or NAIA that might be part of your high school's college night event. Also, any potential college coach who is interested in working with you may be a helpful resource to let you know what paperwork you need to have in place to make you eligible. Just like the admission process, there are deadlines so be sure to start early. You don't want to miss out on any great opportunities.

PERFORMING ARTS AUDITIONS

Students who need to audition for anything arts-related that involves music (vocals and instrument) and performing (acting, dance, etc.) need to jump through an extra hoop in the college admission process. In addition to being chosen academically for admission, there needs to be a match artistically. If you are a tuba player and are set on playing at the college level whether for a marching band or orchestra, you must find a college that 1) needs a tuba player and 2) thinks you are the best tuba player they can get. To do this, get yourself in front of as many people that need a fill-in-the-blank (tuba player, dancer, actor, etc.) so you can increase your chances of being chosen.

One way of doing this might include having video of your performances that can be sent to the potential college (including links that can be sent for YouTube videos if they request it). This allows the decision-makers to see your talent without necessarily seeing you in person. This is not ideal, however, and most colleges I have talked to prefer in-person auditions. For in-person auditions, you will contact the schools in which you are interested to find out when their audition dates will be. This is most likely during the first semester of your senior year in high school but may run all the way up to February of your senior year. This is time-consuming in that it requires you to audition one school at a time. However, it does usually mean a smaller pool of candidates and a more intimate setting.

When you attend an individual school's audition, it does require a great deal of research and staying on top of deadlines and dates so you know when the auditions will be taking place. You will need to do your homework in advance to know what schools' auditions you will want to attend and have a well-orchestrated schedule in place. If you are a theater performer, you have a second option for auditioning that broadens your audience, and that is to do a national unified audition. In this scenario, regional auditions are held that a student can attend. At this event, there may be several different colleges and universities present who are looking for talent. To find a unified audition in your part of the country, you can go to www.unifiedauditions.com for a list of cities and dates. There you can also find a list of colleges and universities who participate in the National Unified Auditions program.

Another venue for visual and performing arts students to connect with potential colleges might be through a college fair designed specifically for visual and performing arts majors. The National Association for College Admissions Counseling (NACAC) sponsors fairs around the country that invite colleges with visual and performing arts programs to meet with potential students in a college fair format. While there is no auditioning that takes place at these events, it gives students and their families the opportunity to meet and ask questions about programs, auditions, and other arts-related topics. There are over 20 national college fairs sponsored by NACAC that are geared specifically to students in the visual and performing arts. These fairs are usually held in the fall. For more information on NACAC Visual and Performing Arts fairs, go to www.nacacfairs.org/attend/pva/.

Just like athletes, performers should have a backup plan in the event they are not picked up by a college or university for performing arts. A second wish list indicating schools that are potential fits without the performing arts piece is a smart idea. You may have a school that is your number one choice based on the performing arts program, but if you were not in the performing arts program, it wouldn't make the list at all. Remember the advice about not putting all your eggs in one basket? This is a perfect example.

ART MAJORS

If you are considering majoring in art, you will need to submit a portfolio of your work that may include photos, sketches, video, and/or clips of your work depending upon your interest area as well as the specific requirements of the college's art program. You will most likely use SlideRoom, a portfolio platform, to upload and submit your work. Educate yourself about how portfolio submission works so you have a clear understanding of what you will need to do. Work with your art teacher from early in your high school career to produce and then choose your best pieces for submission as part of your portfolio. A portfolio should ideally be developed over time and not something you rush to throw together at the last minute.

STUDENTS WITH LEARNING DISABILITIES AND DIFFERENCES

Students who face challenges in the classroom due to a diagnosed learning disability will also need to look at college programs carefully to see how they might provide accommodations to help them succeed. Colleges with disability program services used to be limited. Now they are widespread, and you'd be hard-pressed to find a school that doesn't offer some services. Services, though, can come in a wide variety of packages ranging from tutoring and writing centers to extremely structured programs to help a student learn and succeed at the college level.

The first thing I would encourage students and parents to do here is to be honest about what the student truly needs to succeed. Be sure to share the diagnosis with the school you are interested in pursuing. This will help them provide an honest assessment of what services they can provide and whether their school can truly provide the assistance a student will need. As an example, if a student has been receiving accommodations at the high school level for a reading disability and has been receiving extended time on tests or having instructions read to them it would be important for parents and the student to ask if the college or university also provides these accommodations. This assumes, of course, the student has been receiving them at his or her high school AND he or she has the proper documentation from a qualified professional or district outlining the assessments the child was given and the diagnosis resulting from those assessments.

If you've somehow managed to get special accommodations at the high school level without proper documentation, you've just been lucky. A doctor writing a note on a prescription pad is not enough. Colleges will need FULL documentation from a psychologist, neurologist, special education testing program through the school district, or another qualified professional that outlines exactly what testing and assessments were completed to determine the diagnosis. Chances are if a student has had a learning issue, it's been going on for a long time and taking steps to get help should have happened long before now. Getting Johnny tested in his junior year because you'd like to see him get extended time accommodations on his ACT or SAT is not a good reason. Testing programs require documentation and special accommodation paperwork as do colleges. If you've been through disability diagnostic assessments previously and your information is up-to-date (within the last three years), you should be good to go.

The second thing I would recommend you look at is the structure and depth of any student service program for students with learning differences. This means you will need to dig and dig deep. If you ask a simple question like "does your school have a program for students with ADHD?" and the answer from them is "Yes," what you need to do is press on and ask more about the services they provide and for how long. It's one thing to say you have a program, but how you structure it is completely different. Is their support in the form of a learning center the student must self-initiate to use or is it a situation where they are required to meet weekly with an adviser? Is it a 'freshman only' program or does it grow with them each subsequent year, so they have support all the way through until graduation? Are their professors notified of the student's learning disability at the beginning of the semester, so they know from the start what the circumstances are? Asking a lot of questions and physically seeing these offices on the campus are the only ways you are going to have a better idea of what services are offered. Sticking a writing center in the back corner of a library will do little to ensure the success of a quiet student who might lack the self-confidence or self-advocacy skills to use them by his or her own volition.

If you are looking for people to help you in the college process as it relates to learning disability services, you might consider asking a special education teacher, learning specialist, or counselor at school for their advice. They may have suggestions on what questions they would ask, what services they think the student would benefit from, and even schools they have knowledge of that have strong programs for students with learning disabilities. These professionals know the student better than anyone, and their personal knowledge of a student's learning style can be so helpful in potentially matching them with the right college and/or services. Their expertise in the field can pay off here if you solicit help and ask for their opinion, but it will be your job as a family to start asking a lot of questions early in the student's high school career to make sure you don't get left behind or get a late start.

If you don't have any one person at the high school level who can assist you with your questions, you might check out book resources on the subject to determine what colleges even offer specialized programs for students with a learning difference. One of those books, *The K&W Guide to Colleges for Students with Learning Differences,* is a go-to favorite of many college counselors I know. You can buy it online or at bookstores, and it's available for anyone to purchase.

There are several books on the topic of learning differences. This is only one of many options you might want to read.

Regardless of how you choose to gather your information, remember to first always seek the help of professionals who are knowledgeable of your situation and/or college programs. Secondly, always be armed with an abundance of questions to dig deep. You will find throughout the college process that the more proactive you are, the better the college search process will go.

ACTION STEPS
for Chapter 12

SPECIAL CIRCUMSTANCES

GAP YEAR:

1) Apply to colleges as though you would not be doing a gap year.

2) Educate yourself on gap year options by reading books, checking gap year websites, and investigating programs.

3) Decide on costs you are willing to pay if attending a formal gap year program.

4) Enlist the help of a counselor to plan your gap year if you will not be doing a formal program.

ATHLETICS:

1) Keep grades up (all four years).

2) Register with NCAA Eligibility Center (Division I or II) or NAIA Eligibility Center by the end of junior year.

3) Send 6-semester high school transcript to eligibility center at the end of junior year.

4) Send ACT/SAT scores to NCAA or NAIA eligibility centers.

5) Keep accurate track of athletic statistics and game video in case potential recruiters ask for it.

ACTION STEPS
for Chapter 12

SPECIAL CIRCUMSTANCES

PERFORMING ARTS:

1) Consider having video available that showcases your talent.

2) Contact colleges to see when their individual auditions are held on their campuses.

3) If you are an actor, look into National Unified Auditions to see when and where regional auditions will be held

4) Consider attending a NACAC-sponsored Visual Performing Arts college fair.

ART MAJORS:

1) Work with your art teacher from early in your high school career to choose key pieces you've created for your portfolio.

2) Education yourself as to what is required for submission for each college's program.

3) Become familiar with portfolio submission programs such as SlideRoom which allow you to upload and submit your portfolio as part of the application process.

ACTION STEPS
for Chapter 12

SPECIAL CIRCUMSTANCES

LEARNING DIFFERENCES:

1) Have all your diagnoses formally documented by a qualified clinician and make sure your reports are up-to-date.

2) Seek ACT and/or SAT special accommodations well in advance of upcoming test dates. (Ask for help from your school counselor to do this.)

3) Enlist the expertise of school counselor, special education teacher, or other high school professionals who can help you find the best special services fit possible.

4) Explore options of available programs at various colleges and universities including structure and depth of services offered.

5) Be sure to VISIT and ask a lot of questions regarding services provided.

Glossary of Terms

2-YEAR EDUCATION (ASSOCIATE DEGREE): This usually means community college or a trade or technical college. Community colleges offer associate degrees. They may be in a specific career field that the student may enter directly after graduation (vet tech, occupational therapy assistant, etc.). Other students opt to get their associate degree in a general transfers major which allows them to get their foundation courses (English, math, social studies, science) and then transfer them to a four-year school to complete their bachelor degree there.

4-YEAR EDUCATION (BACHELOR DEGREE): This means a traditional college. Students who graduate from here have a four-year degree (bachelor) and its sets them up for professional entry level jobs (nursing, teaching, business, engineering, etc.). Many students like the traditional four-year education because they want to have a chance to experience college life in its truest sense. Depending upon location, students can either live at home and commute or live in student housing when attending a four-year school.

529 SAVINGS PLAN: A tax-advantaged savings plan that allows families to save and invest money for college. Anyone can start a 529 plan for a student. 529 programs are recognized by the government and IRS. 529 plans can be run by states or agencies as well as educational institutions. There are many 529 plans available. Do your homework before you invest so you choose the right plan for you.

ACT: (American College Testing) Standardized college entrance exam that test students in four areas: English, Math, Reading, and Science. A composite (overall) score is awarded in addition to the subject areas. These scores are used as part of the decision-making and course placement process for many colleges. The ACT score range is 1-36.

ACTIVITY LIST (OR RESUME): This is a comprehensive and concise list of activities in which the student has participated either in or out of school during grades 9-12.

The activity list should detail a student's contribution to a given club, sport, or other activity to give the college or university a clear understanding of the student's involvement, talents, and interests outside of the classroom.

ADMISSIONS REPRESENTATIVE: Each college has a specific individual assigned to a specific high school or geographic region. Your admission rep is there to help answer your admission and scholarship questions as well as be an advocate in the admission process for you. Knowing your admission rep throughout the admission process can be a big help to you. Make sure you know the admission rep at each school to which you are applying.

ADVANCED PLACEMENT (AP): Advanced Placement courses allow students to enroll in a college-level standardized curriculum class taught at the high school level. An Advanced Placement exam is offered at the end of the term and, depending upon the student's score, may award the student college level credit for the course. What score is needed for the student to be offered college level credit varies from college to college. A student does not need to have been enrolled in an AP course to be able to sit for an AP exam. AP score ranges are from 1-5.

COLLEGE: An institution of higher learning for post-secondary (after high school) students. Colleges will offer either 2-year or 4-year degrees. Associate degrees (2-year degrees) are usually awarded by community colleges while bachelor degrees are offered by 4-year colleges. Traditional and liberal arts colleges focus on mainly undergraduate (4-year degrees). The terms "college" and "university" are often used interchangeably.

COMMON APPLICATION: An admission application that is accepted at approximately 700 different colleges and universities. Using the Common Application allows a student to complete one application and submit it to several schools rather than filling out each school's individual online application.

COST OF ATTENDANCE (COA): The total bill to attend a college. This includes tuition, room and board, books, and fees.

DEPARTMENTAL SCHOLARSHIP: Money that is awarded to a student for enrolling in a specific major.

DIRECT ENTRY: A process where a student is admitted to their chosen major as a freshman and doesn't have to apply to their program (and potentially be rejected) at a later point in college.

DUAL ENROLLMENT: The act of being enrolled in a high school level course that also offers college credit. An example of this is a student being awarded high school credit for a class taken at the high school while also receiving credit simultaneously at the college level for enrolling in the course. Most dual enrollment courses award college credit from a specific university though that credit may be transferred to another university upon graduation from high school.

EARLY ACTION: Students who apply using this admission policy option will have an earlier deadline than those who apply during a regular application season. However, they will also receive their admission decision earlier than the regular application pool. Students who apply under early action are not required to attend the institution if they are accepted.

EARLY DECISION: An admission procedure (policy) that some colleges use in their admission process. Students choosing this option are bound to a specific school if admitted and must withdraw all other applications if they are admitted under early decision. This will require students commit to their university well in advance of the May 1 National Reply Date.

EXPECTED FAMILY CONTRIBUTION (EFC): This is the dollar amount the family is expected to pay towards a student's education after the FAFSA has been completed and all the number-crunching has been done. A family's EFC may vary from year to year based on the filing of a new FAFSA if the family's financial status has changed.

FAFSA: Free Application for Federal Student Aid. This is a government form that must be completed in the fall of a student's senior year to be considered for federal financial aid (grants, loans, etc.). This is for need-based aid only and not scholarships.

FERPA: Family Education Rights and Privacy Act. As part of FERPA legislation, **students who are over the age of 18 and enrolled in a post-secondary institution have their personal information protected so parents cannot see their child's grades.** In many cases, a student may go to the registrar's office at their college and sign a waiver allowing their parents to receive their grades if the parents request it. Colleges are obligated to notify parents and students annually of their rights under FERPA.

FINANCIAL AID: Monetary assistance that is given to a student to finance their education. Financial aid can come in the form of loans or grants and is based on student need. Loans will need to be repaid and grants will not. Scholarships are another form of aid but are based on merit and do NOT need to be repaid.

GAP YEAR: A period of time (usually about 12 months) that a student takes away from academic life between high school graduation and the first year of college. Students often use this time to do service, work, travel, learn a new language, or have other immersion experiences. The purpose of a gap year is to promote personal growth and make students better prepared to enroll in college.

GRANTS: Money a student is awarded from a college that does NOT need to be repaid. It is essentially a "gift."

HONORS COLLEGE: A special program offered by some colleges and universities that allow students to enroll in more challenging classes at the college level. These classes often offer more in-depth curriculum, smaller classes, and special projects and speakers. Some honors programs offer enrolled students preferential treatment including special housing and early registration. Students who complete the honors college program will often receive distinction on their transcripts or at graduation.

INFORMATIONAL INTERVIEWS: The process of spending time talking with someone about their profession. Informational interviews help people who are seeking information on a given career path to determine if this line of work may be a good fit for them.

JOB SHADOWING: Observing a specific career in the workplace with the purpose of gaining information regarding the job to make an informed career decision. Job shadowing often gives people an up-close and real-life example of the day-to-day activities required to do a specific job.

LEGACY: Legacy is when the applicant has a relative (grandparent, parent, sibling) who has attended the university before them. This can also be helpful in some admission processes.

LIBERAL ARTS COLLEGE: Focuses on the breadth of education and teaching students critical thinking skills. Their emphasis is largely focused on problem-solving ability and you will often find writing and public speaking woven throughout the curriculum. Liberal arts colleges can be public or private.

NAIA ELIGIBILITY: The process of becoming athletically and academically eligible to play NAIA sports in college. Students should file with the NAIA Eligibility Center by the end of their junior year to determine their eligibility to play college sports at the NAIA level.

NATIONAL MERIT: National Merit is a scholarship program offered through the PSAT to students who have taken the PSAT as a junior. Top scorers may be offered the distinction of semi-finalist, finalist, or commended student. Money may be awarded to the top scoring students and funded by National Merit Corporation or corporate sponsors. In addition, some colleges offer scholarship packages to those with National Merit distinction.

NATIONAL REPLY DATE: This is the date each year by which every high school senior must commit to one school and notify the others to which they applied they will not be coming. The national reply date is May 1.

NCAA ELIGIBILITY: The process of becoming athletically and academically eligible to play NCAA Division I or II sports in college. Students should file with the NCAA Eligibility Center by the end of their junior year to determine their eligibility to play college sports at these divisions.

NET PRICE CALCULATOR (NPC): Found on each college's website, the net price calculator estimates the cost for a student to attend a specific college for a single year after scholarships and financial aid not needing to be repaid are deducted.

PERSONALITY INVENTORY: This type of assessment gives insight to personality attributes one possesses that can help identify strengths and provide information on how one may work best and with whom as well as provide insight on careers that may be a good fit.

PLAN / PRE-ACT / ASPIRE: These tests are pre-ACT tests offered by ACT. Results from these tests will predict student's future score ranges for the actual ACT. These scores do not count towards the student's entrance exam requirement for college. They are designed to help students prepare for future ACT's and give a predicted score for the ACT to help students plan.

PRIVATE COLLEGE: Private institutions are funded by tuition as well as private donors and are not supplemented by tax dollars. Private schools can be religiously affiliated, but many are without ties to a specific religion.

PSAT: Preliminary Scholastic Aptitude Test. This test is offered during the student's junior year in high school (in October). Results from this test predict the student's future SAT score. Scores from the student's junior year PSAT may qualify them for National Merit Scholarship competition.

PUBLIC COLLEGE: Funded by state and federal tax dollars. While there is still tuition at public schools, the sticker price is often much lower than private institutions. Public schools tend to have larger enrollment but that, too, is not always the case.

ROLLING ADMISSION: A common admission policy used by many colleges and universities whereby applications are processed as they are received and admission decisions go out in the same fashion. Colleges using a rolling admissions policy may still have deadlines the students must make for priority consideration such as housing and scholarship. Overall, though, rolling admission allows students a larger time frame in which to apply.

ROTC: (Reserve Officers' Training Corps) A college program at some universities that prepare students to serve as officers in the military after graduation. College costs are covered in exchange for military service after graduation. Check with each school and branch of the military to find out more on obligations and financial awards within their specific programs.

SAT: (Scholastic Aptitude Test) Standardized college entrance exam that test students in Critical Reading (English) and Mathematics. An overall score is awarded in addition to the subject areas. These scores are used as part of the decision-making and course placement process for many colleges. The SAT score range is 400-1600.

SAT SUBJECT AREA TESTS: These are individual tests that MAY be required by some colleges as part of the admission process in addition to the SAT. To see a list of subject tests offered, go to the Collegeboard website.

SCHOLARSHIPS: Money that is awarded to a student for merit. Merit may be academic, leadership, athletic, etc. This money is often given by the college itself or a student may apply for and receive merit money from private organizations to be used towards college costs. Scholarship money does not need to be repaid. Some scholarships are renewable (meaning they can be used in subsequent years) assuming the criteria for keeping the scholarship is met (GPA, attendance, etc.).

SLIDEROOM: A program that allows art students to upload and submit portfolios of their work to colleges for review in the admission process.

STACKING: When a student is allowed to put one scholarship award on top of another without any reduction in award. As an example, if a student is awarded $10,000 from a university and can add private scholarship money ON TOP OF that, this is what we call stacking. (Stacking is a good thing!)

SINGLE CHOICE EARLY ACTION (ALSO KNOWN AS RESTRICTIVE EARLY ACTION): This program works the same as early action—students have an earlier deadline to submit their application but find out their admission decision earlier and are not obligated to attend if admitted. However, under Single Choice, the student may only apply early action to ONE institution.

STUDENT LOANS: Money that is given to a student to finance his or her education. This money will need to be repaid with interest.

STUDY ABROAD: Programs offered by colleges that allow students to study (usually a semester) in a foreign country. Some schools have campuses of their own in different countries while some have exchange programs with foreign colleges and universities. Costs can vary widely from being included in tuition costs (travel is not usually covered) to being an additional cost to the student. Be sure to ask what costs are incurred for study abroad.

SUPER-SCORING: A process where a college takes the highest subject score from different test dates of the ACT and/or SAT and creates a new, higher composite score. Doing this helps students in the admission and scholarship process. Not all schools super score. Ask your admission representative if their school super scores.

TEST OPTIONAL: Schools that do not require standardized tests (ACT or SAT) as part of the admission application are known as test optional schools. These schools require other information such as essays, transcripts, interviews, and other data to make a student's admission decision.

TRANSCRIPT: This is essentially an academic snapshot of a student's record. In addition to student's demographic information like name, address, gender, and date of birth, a transcript likely includes names of courses, semester grades, credit earned and attendance. Transcripts may or may not contain standardized test scores depending on the school's policy.

UNIFIED AUDITIONS: These auditions are held annually in several cities across the U.S. for students who want to audition for theater performance at various colleges. Several colleges will be in attendance at one location allowing a student to audition in front of several colleges at once versus having to audition at each school individually.

UNIVERSITY: An institution of higher learning for post-secondary (after high school) students. In addition to 4-year (undergraduate) degrees, universities also offer a number of graduate and post-graduate programs (Master and Doctoral degrees). The terms "college" and "university" are often used interchangeably.

WAITLIST: A process where a college or university has neither denied nor granted the student admission. Colleges have waitlists to fill any empty spots they may have after applicants have declined admission. In the event a spot becomes available, a student may then be moved off the waitlist and admitted to the freshman class. Offers to move off the waitlist can often happen after the May 1 deadline. Colleges do not necessarily go to their waitlists every year and not all colleges use a waitlist policy as part of their admission process.

Helpful Websites

CAREER INTEREST INVENTORIES:
www.onetonline.org (Free)

www.self-directed-search.com (Pay)

COLLEGE SEARCH ENGINES:
Big Future: www.bigfuture.collegeboard.com

Princeton Review: www.princetonreview.com

Cappex: www.cappex.com

Niche: www.niche.com/?ref=colleges

Chegg (Zinch): www.chegg.com/schools

Fast Web: www.fastweb.com/

Peterson's: www.petersons.com

COMMON APPLICATION:
www.commonapp.org

EMPLOYMENT WEBSITES:
www.indeed.com

www.linkedin.com

FEDERAL APPLICATION FOR FEDERAL STUDENT AID (FAFSA):
www.fafsa.ed.gov

GAP YEAR:
www.guides.teenlife.com/gap

www.americangap.org

NATIONWIDE PERFORMANCE AUDITIONS AND COLLEGE FAIRS:
www.unifiedauditions.com

www.nacacfairs.org/attend/pva/

PERSONALITY INVENTORY:
www.16personalities.com (Free)

PLAYING COLLEGE SPORTS:
www.elgibilitycenter.org (NCAA)

www.playnaia.org (NAIA)

REGISTERING FOR COLLEGE FAIRS:
www.gotocollegefairs.com

www.strivefair.com

TEST OPTIONAL SCHOOLS:
www.fairtest.org

TEST PREP AND REGISTRATION:
www.act.org

www.collegeboard.com

VOLUNTEER WEBSITES:
www.volunteermatch.org

www.volunteerodyssey.com (Memphis community)

www.nationalservice.gov/programs/americorps

www.catholicvolunteernetwork.org

www.pointsoflight.org/handsonnetwork

www.idealist.org

VIDEO SUBMISSION:
www.zeemee.com

MORE ON THE AUTHOR:
www.cct-stl.com

Suggested Books to Read

Gap to Great by Andrea Wien

Where You Go Is Not Who'll You'll Be by Frank Bruni

Colleges That Change Lives by Loren Pope

The K&W Guide to Colleges for Students with Learning Differences by Marybeth Kravets and Imy Wax

Do What You Are by Paul D. Tieger

Closing Thoughts

I hope that you have found this book to be helpful in starting your journey to college. Whether you are a parent trying to help your son or daughter or a high school student wanting to figure it all out, I hope this book was a great starting point and will be a step in the right direction. Knowledge is power! Above all else, I hope you take to heart the message that college is all about FIT and everyone has a path and a plan unique to their own talents, abilities, and situation. Like I said in the beginning, run your own race. Find your FIT. Listen to your gut. Follow the steps listed in this book. Plan ahead. Meet deadlines. Work hard. Do your best. Enlist the help of others. If you can do these things, the rest will fall into place.

My favorite quote comes from Henry David Thoreau and seems appropriate as a final thought for this book:

"Go confidently in the direction of your dreams.
Live the life you have imagined."

Be well. Enjoy the journey.

> If you need extra help along the way and would like to contact me regarding consultation appointments (in person or remote), speaking engagements, or workshops, please contact me at joann@cct-stl.com or call 314-384-3134. You can also learn more at www.cct-stl.com. Volume order pricing for books is available. Please check the website for more information.

Acknowledgements

Whenever I would glance at the Acknowledgement section of any book I would read, I wouldn't quite get it. I mean, the author did all the work. Why in the world were so many people involved? Now that I have taken on this task of writing a book for the first time, I totally get it. Just like enlisting people to help with the college process, I needed to ask for help so many times for various aspects of this project. This project would not have been possible without the many friends I entrusted with my idea and who told me I could do this, pushed me to see it through, and verified it was a topic on which people wanted and needed more information. There were many friends (and, in some cases, their kids) who read the manuscript over and over and gave me feedback from a parent perspective, a student perspective, and a college rep perspective. They believed in what I was doing and wanted to be a part of helping me reach my goal. There are my crazy former co-workers who keep me going and keep me laughing. Thanks for all you do to make education such a wonderful experience for so many students. Special thanks to my good friend Laura who did the initial edits to this book and to my wonderful, amazing, and supportive husband, Brian, who believed in me every step of the way. Thanks to all of you for believing in me and my mission to help people better their lives through education, hard work, and a belief in themselves. By doing our personal best and finding our purpose in life, we all contribute to making this world a better place. And that, my friends, is a win-win for the universe.

Made in the USA
Columbia, SC
14 August 2019